LOVE DATED

39 Multicultural Dates

WHAT I LEARNED ABOUT
LOVE, IDENTITY & DESIRE

NIA YARA

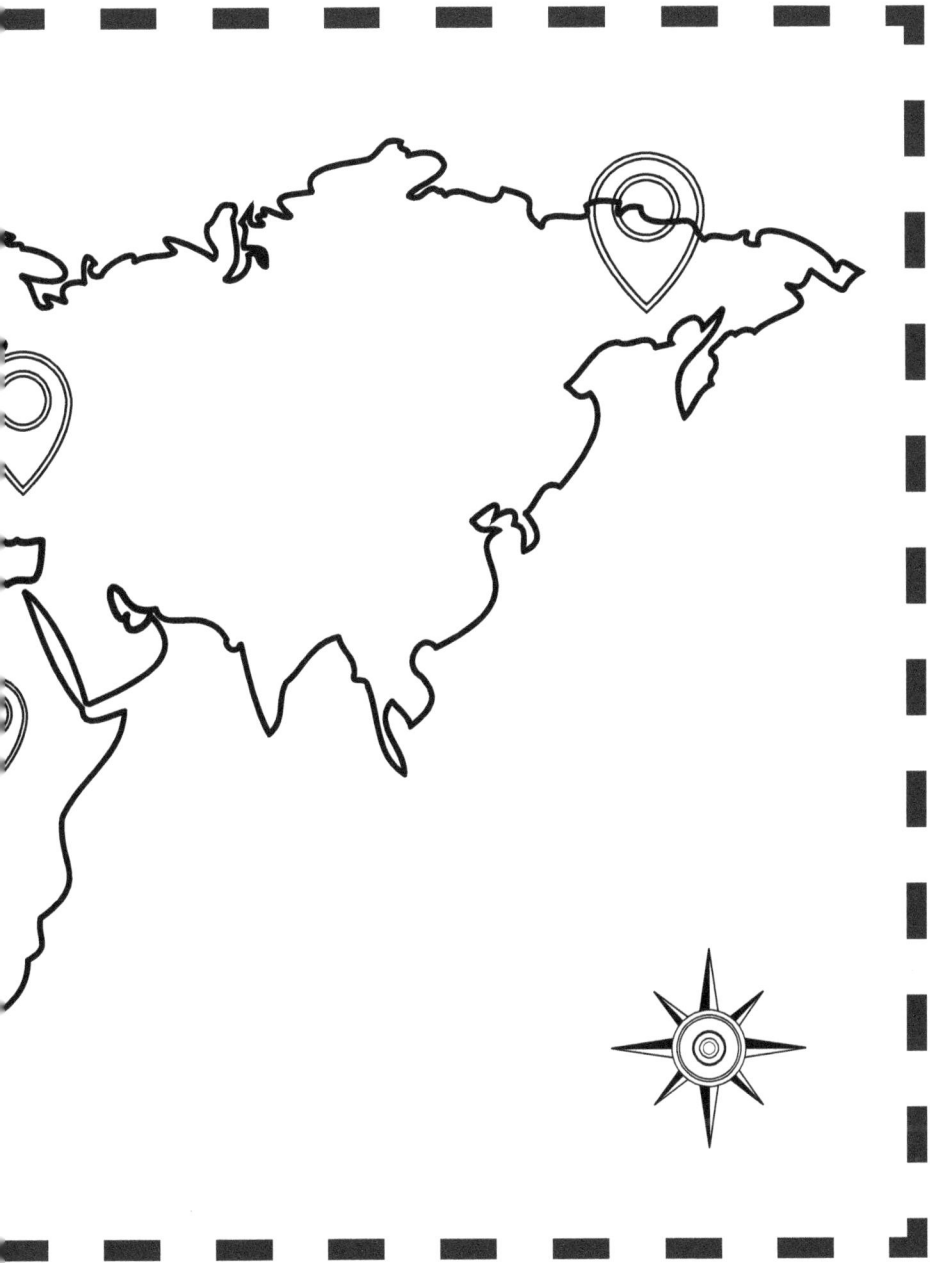

NIA YARA

Love [DATED] a Memoir
39 Multicultural Dates
What I Learned About Love Identity & Desire
Published in English, Portuguese, and Spanish by Nia Yara – www. NiaYara.com
This book is a work of nonfiction based on real experiences.

First Edition 2025
ISBN: 978-1-0695783-6-5

Dedication

To the Amazon,
here standing for Mother Nature herself,
wild, wise, and wounded,
thank you for holding me through every transformation.

To all women,
who carry generations in their bodies
and revolutions in their silence.

And to you,
my partner in life and in soul,
who stood beside me through every chapter,
more than anything, thank you for your courage to let me
write.
I love you.

Contents

Preface: The Dating Anthropologist   13
The Field: Welcome to Toronto – The Lab   15
Note on Cultural Glimpses   23
Chapter 0: The Safety (and You) First   25
Safety Is a Love Language   27
You're Not a Supporting Character   29
For the Ones Reading Closely   31
Date 1 - Ryan: The Celtic Experiment   33
Date 2 - Rohan: Bon Jovi Land   37
Date 3 - Allan: The Croatian Spectrum   41
Date 4 - Casey: A Lesson in Sensuality and Vietnamese Culture
    45
Date 5 - Jason: Mr. Maple Leaf   49
Date 6 - Alex: A Mediterranean Lesson in Freedom   53
Date 7 - Sean: The Irish with a Broken Heart   57
Date 8 - Jace: The Canadian Soulander   61
Date 9 - Dani: The Aussie with Two Baby Mamas and Two Stories
    65
Date 10 - Ewan: The Scottish Riddle Man   69
Date 11 - Joe: The Sicilian Exorcism   73
Date 12 - Armen: The Armenian Dream Husband   77
Date 13 - Ali: The Afghan-German Drift   81
Date 14 - Savvas: The Greek Sphinx   83
Date 15 - Sri: @Virgen29 - The Uniform of Grace   87
Date 16 - Steve: The Man from the North   91
Date 17 - Mike: The Roman Gravedigger of Chaos   95
Date 18 - Daniel: The Portuguese Historian   99
Date 19 - David: The Dominican Chef   103
Date 20 - Luca: The Perfect MapleMan for that Perfect Picture
    107

Date 21 - Stephen: The Scottish McHusband   111
Date 22 - Carlos: The Salvadorian Almost Love   115
Date 23 - Rajesh: The Pakistani Diva   119
Date 24 - Simone: The French Connection   123
Chapter 1 – Awakening: Coexistability   127
Date 25 - Maurice: The French Canadian Divorcee   131
Date 26 - Stephan: The Nigerian Sweet Talker   135
Date 27 - Jack: The Jamaican Poet   139
Date 28 - Osmani: The Cuban Revolutionary of Love   143
Date 29 - Darius: The Persian D-Pic Guy   147
Date 30 - Adrian: The Romanian Spell   151
Date 31 - Aoi: The Japanese Ritualist   155
Date 32 - Rakesh: The Indian In-Between   159
Date 33 - Marx: The Native Signal   163
Date 34 - Victor: The Argentinian Hermano, Pero no Mucho
                                                          167
Date 35 - Marco: The Italo-Canadian Firefighter   171
Date 36 - Izidoro: The Italian Things We Just Can't Help 175
Date 37 - Valentin: The Berlin Wall and the Bear   179
Date 38 - Phillip: A Polish Illusion of a Dream   183
Date 39 - Michael: The Israeli Paradox   187
Chapter 40 - Simone: Th3 Black Cat   191
The 40° LOVE - Becoming   195
Epilogue: Meow...   199
Note on Discussion Guide   201
Discussion Guide   202
   Educator's Discussion Guide: Gender, Power, and the Politics of
Love   203
   Guia de Discussão para Educadores: Gênero, Poder e a Política do
Amor   210
   Guía de Discusión para Educadores: Género, Poder y la Política del
Amor   217

"One is not born, but rather becomes, a woman.

Simone de Beauvoir

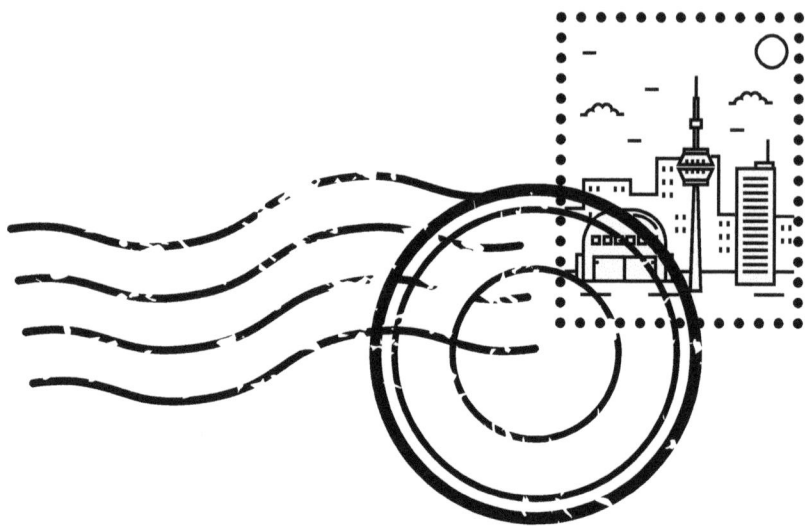

Preface
The Dating Anthropologist

I moved to Toronto with more questions than plans. That was my nature—to follow curiosity like a compass. Curiosity was and always has been the direction I've taken. Not north. Not marriage. Just toward something true.

I've always been an observer. I'm a social scientist by training but an anthropologist by instinct. I don't look at people to judge them—I look to understand. I want to know what makes people stay, what makes them leave, what makes us ache, and what makes us bloom.

Dating became my research.

Not for a thesis but for a self I hadn't fully met yet.

I fell in love with accents, stories, ideas. I studied the subtle dialects of touch and timing. I wasn't searching for the one—I was learning how to become the many parts of me I'd left behind or never dared to be.

Each man became a page in that study. A scent. A metaphor. A portal. Some were unforgettable. Some were unforgivable. All of them revealed something.

About power. About softness. About longing and its limits.

This isn't a book about happily ever after.

It's about what happened before—the beautiful, messy, electric before.

Because to find a love worth choosing, I had to meet the versions of myself that said yes, no, maybe, never again.

And then, eventually, the one who whispered: now.

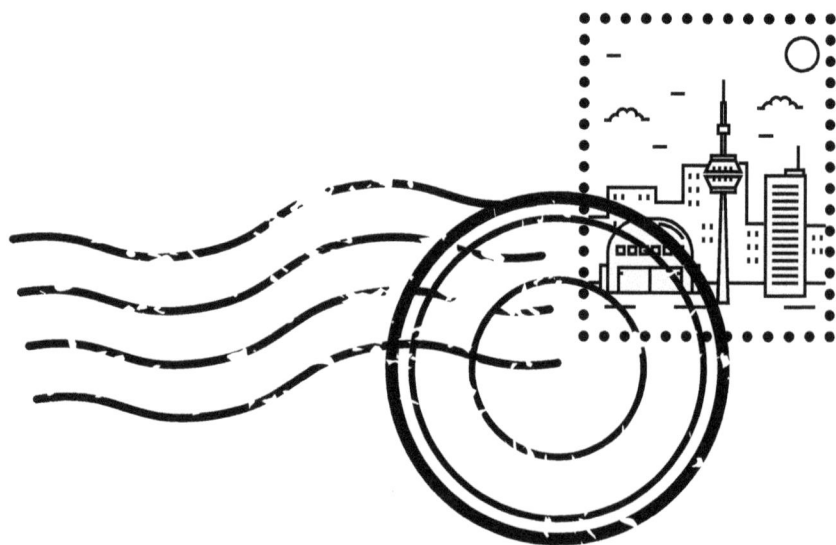

The Field
Welcome to Toronto - The Lab

"Toronto was my lab. The world, my curriculum."

I was lying in the grass at Todmorden Mills Park, book on my belly, sunlight flickering through the leaves like secrets. Summer in Toronto carries a particular kind of nostalgia. You don't know what for exactly, but you feel it—something you've almost lived, but not quite. Like the winter has never existed and summer will never end.

I had a black cat beside me—yes, a real one. She's not just a metaphor. Though soon she would become one. Her fur shimmered like ink in the sun, her body curled around my thigh like she owned me. And maybe she did. I called her my totem. My shadow self. My intuition made flesh and fur.

We were watching people—couples, mostly. A man playing with his toddler. A girl journaling under a tree. Two teenagers in a tango of pretending not to flirt. The park was quiet, but buzzing in a way only summer can be. I pressed my thumb between the pages of my book, letting it breathe. The words blurred.

This is where the idea began to form. Not in a rush. Not in a heartbreak. Not in a moment of rage or orgasm or feminist enlightenment. But in this slow, breathing space.

I have loved a lot of men and a few women. But more than that, I had observed them. Witnessed them. Sat across them in late-night diners and busy cafés and beds that still smelled of foreign laundry detergent.

This book is not a tell-all. It is a tell-why. It's not revenge. Not judgment. Not a BuzzFeed listicle. And certainly not a user's manual for how to date or avoid heartbreak.

It is, quite simply, a field study. Conducted on the urban savannah of Toronto, across cultures, accents, dating apps, algorithms, taxi rides, and long walks home. Because Toronto is not just a city—it's a globe in miniature. You don't date a "Canadian" here. You date an Afghan-German, a Cuban revolutionary, a Portuguese historian, a First Nations healer, a Dominican single father raising three daughters. You date Jamaica, Vietnam, Japan, Nigeria. You date migration itself.

You don't just date either. You date families. Ghosts. Political systems. You date inherited trauma. Colonial residue. Catholic guilt. Post-divorce tenderness. You date the women who raised them, the boys they used to be, the borders they've crossed. Eventually, you start seeing the patterns. That's what this is. Pattern recognition. Love, as anthropology.

I was a firefighter once. Did I mention that? Strange job for a feminist romantic, I know. But it taught me things. How to be calm inside chaos. How to know when to enter, and when to retreat. How to read smoke. How to carry weight. That training stayed with me—especially in love. Because people carry weight, too. And some burn from the inside. And sometimes, you walk into a relationship thinking you can save someone, only to find you're the one who needed rescuing.

Later, I worked in healthcare. Ten years. Supporting patients with complex needs, paperwork, trauma, and stubborn systems. I learned to listen without trying to fix. I learned to wait for the real story. Then I went back to school to study social work. I wanted to understand people before they needed saving. I wanted to speak the languages under their silence. And somewhere in between all that—I dated.

There were 39 of them. That I wrote about. There were more, of course, but those 39 taught me something. They were my curriculum. Some were chapters. Some, footnotes. A few, entire courses. Each one is a story. A man. A culture. A lesson. A mirror. You'll meet them all.

There was Alex, the polyamorous philosopher with the emerald gaze and impossible timing. Simone, his wife—an elegant French woman who changed my understanding of partnership in three quiet encounters.

There was Ryan, the Celtic Viking with a soft core and a terminal illness.

David, the Dominican chef, raising daughters with the kind of tenderness most men aren't taught.

Darius, who sent me unsolicited photos and taught me how to confront a digital predator with dignity, not shame.

Jason, Mr. Maple Leaf, who reminded me what steadfastness looks like.

Osmani, the Cuban who turned seduction into survival.

Victor, the Argentine football fan who sparked a Brazil-vs.-Argentina showdown in my own hormones.

Marco, the Italian firefighter whose presence was so cinematic that I had to take notes just to believe it was real.

I changed most of their names. Not because I needed to protect them. Because this book isn't about them. It's about what they reflected back to me.

When I first told my partner I was writing this book, he raised an eyebrow. "Isn't it a little... intimate?" he asked.

It was. But not in the way he feared. I wasn't writing it to expose my past. I was writing it to frame it. To understand it. He wasn't jealous, exactly. Just worried. That I would be misunderstood. That people would reduce me to a "serial dater" or a "man-hater." That the complexity would be flattened. But this book is not for flat minds. It's for the ones willing to think in layers. To feel deeply. To get a little uncomfortable.

He, my partner, is not the prize at the end of the story. He is the witness to its value. No matter what life has for us—he was worth it. Our love was worth it. A Viking who found an Amazonian mermaid. Not in a fairytale. But in the messy, sexy, sacred middle of it all.

I didn't write this book to teach you how to love. I wrote it to show you how I did. How I failed. How I learned. How I stopped waiting for permission. If it helps you on your path, I am honored. If it simply makes you feel seen, or laughed with, or gently challenged—then I've done my job.

This book is a love study. Not love as in "forever." But love as in encounter. Love, as in what did this teach me about myself? Love, as in: how many languages can we speak with our hearts before they stop trying to translate themselves into safety? Th3 black cat is already ahead of us.

The first thing you need to know is that I enjoyed dating. Not every moment of it, of course—there were disasters and disappointments, awkward silences, texts that never came, and the occasional date that felt more like a sociological warning sign than a romantic opportunity. But I enjoyed people. I enjoyed being surprised by them.

And when I wasn't surprised, I took notes. Yes, real notes. There's a folder in my old Google Drive, locked and labeled "Love Study – Raw Data." It holds screenshots, voice notes, half-written thoughts recorded after a date on the streetcar home. I wasn't looking to expose anyone. I was collecting stories. Building patterns.

I dated like a cultural anthropologist wearing red lipstick. Not because I was cold, but because I was curious. Every date was a micro--encounter with history, with gender, with migration, with inherited rules.

Why do Dominican men speak so tenderly about their mothers but struggle to speak about their feelings? Why do some European men lead with confidence and others with charm? Why do First Nations men speak softly when they've inherited centuries of silencing? Why do Brazilian men kiss like poets but fear softness as if it were contagious?

I wasn't just dating. I was decoding. And not just them. Me, too. Every date taught me something about the borders I didn't know I had. Where I tightened. Where I wanted to be held. Where I lied to myself. Where I gave too much.

Every man—and woman—acted like a mirror. Some distorted. Others divine. Some too foggy to see anything at all. But all of them were valuable.

This was my method:

- Step into the story.

- Stay long enough to see the pattern.

- Leave when the lesson is clear.

- Write it down.

18

You might think that sounds calculated. It wasn't. I got my heart broken. More than once. I cried over someone who disappeared after a perfect night. I lost sleep trying to decode a text. I changed outfits three times before a first date. I got ghosted. I deleted messages. I Googled "attachment styles" at 2 a.m. I was never above the mess. But I was learning from it. Even when I was spiraling, there was a part of me that stood outside, taking notes. Like, interesting—so this is what longing feels like after four dates and no closure. Or, ah, so this is how loneliness disguises itself as desire when you haven't been touched in a while.

That observer in me—some might call her cold. I call her sacred. She is the keeper of the story. The part of me who will not let chaos go unarchived. She's the one who, when the pain settles, opens the meta-phorical laptop and starts typing:

Date 6 – Alex: Mediterranean Lesson in Freedom

Date 8 – Jace: The Canadian Soulander

Date 28 – Osmani: The Revolutionary of Love

She's the one who whispers, This isn't just heartbreak. This is data. This is art. This is a map. This is a cultural text made of kisses and goodbyes. I didn't realize it at the time, but I was creating a personal ethnography. Of men. Of love. Of myself as a woman becoming.

Each chapter you'll read in this book holds a country, a question, a theme, and a turning point. Some chapters are lighthearted—a flir-tation that passed like summer rain. Some are heavy. They carry the weight of emotional labor, cultural misalignment, or a ghost still haun-ting the edges of my bed. Some men were unforgettable. Some were so forgettable, I only remembered them through the receipts of the meal. But they all offered me something. Even the ones who didn't mean to. Especially the ones who didn't mean to.

I am not the kind of feminist who believes all men are broken. But I do believe most men are untrained in love. Not just romantically—but emotionally. They are not taught how to hold space, how to listen wi-thout fixing, how to be seen in their own vulnerability. And I don't say this with pity. I say this with empathy. Because the world I want to help build—through this book, through my counseling work, through my podcast—is a world where men and women are not adversaries trying to outwit each other on dating apps.

I want a world where a man can say: "I don't know how to do this, but I'm willing to learn." And a woman can say: "I don't need you to save me, but I'll let you witness me." A world where love is not currency or conquest—but curiosity.

Sometimes I wonder what would have happened if I'd never left Brazil. If I had married early, chosen a safe man, had a conventional life. Maybe I'd be someone's wife by now. Maybe I'd be settled. But I wouldn't have written this book. And I wouldn't have become Th3 Black Cat. That's what they eventually began to call me. An avatar. A myth. A name that held mystery and magic. She became my persona— seductive, wise, untamed. She's not the woman who waits. She's the one who knocks. She's the one who asks the questions that burn. She's the one who walks away without bitterness when the answer doesn't match the value.

Th3 Black Cat isn't just me. She's every woman who's ever been told she was too much for wanting more than comfort. She's the woman who stopped apologizing for being curious. She's the one who didn't just date to be loved—she dated to learn.

I didn't plan to write 39 stories. I thought I'd write a few, maybe publish an essay, maybe start a podcast and call it a day. But the stories kept coming. And when I put them all together, I realized what I'd made.

This isn't just a memoir. This is a love study — 39 portraits, 39 paths, 39 clues in the mystery of becoming whole. They don't line up neatly. Love never does. But taken together, they trace a shape. The shape of a woman unlearning shame. The shape of a city speaking many languages. The shape of a heart that stopped asking for permission to be fully alive.

And so, we begin. Not at the end of love. Not at its peak. But in the field. Toronto—the place where I kissed a Jamaican poet under a willow tree, where I held a Scottish man's dreams in my hands like a fragile bird, where I argued with an Argentine like it was foreplay, and where I met a French woman who reminded me that sometimes, it's the woman who teaches you what real partnership feels like.

This is the beginning. A study not of perfect love, but of honest ones. Not of fairy tales, but of field notes. Not of happily-ever-after, but of what it means to meet someone—and yourself—fully.

The black cat stretches. The sun shifts. The story starts. Turn the page. Let's begin the study.

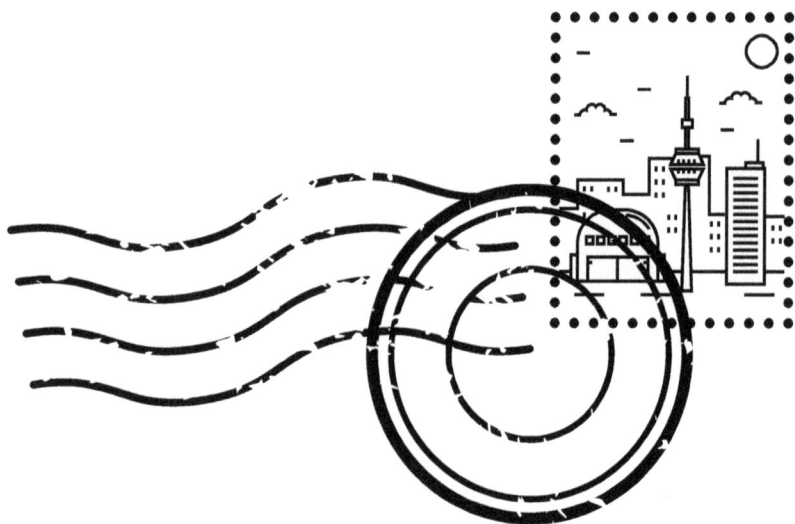

Note on Cultural Glimpses

The cultural glimpses in this book are just that: glimpses. They are personal, partial, and momentary observations, seen through my eyes, my body, and my story. They do not aim to define cultures, countries, or peoples – only to share what I saw, felt, and lived in that fleeting instant.

If you've had similar, different, or complementary experiences, I would love to continue this conversation on my social media. Because culture is alive. And so is love.

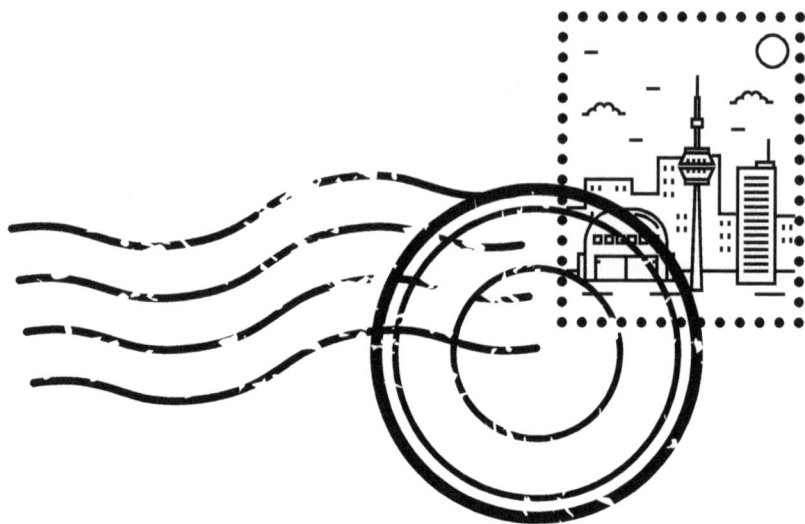

Chapter 0
The Safety (and You) First

Before the first date, the swipe, or the warm pulse of a message that makes you smile—start here. With yourself. With the ground beneath your feet. Not with someone else's opinion of your worth, or your relationship status, or your ability to be loved. But with your own breath. With the sound of your own name in your head, said kindly.

This isn't a manual. You won't find tricks. I've lived some hard stories and some beautiful ones... and I'm still learning. What I offer are pages held open like a hand. I want connection, too. Not at the cost of myself.

Dating can feel like theatre. Lights up. You perform. Your lines are ready. You smile the practiced smile. But you're not on audition on some love reality show (who wants to be part of something that anyway?). You are not here to win a part in someone else's story. You are not a prize. You get to choose. You get to walk in as yourself. And stay.

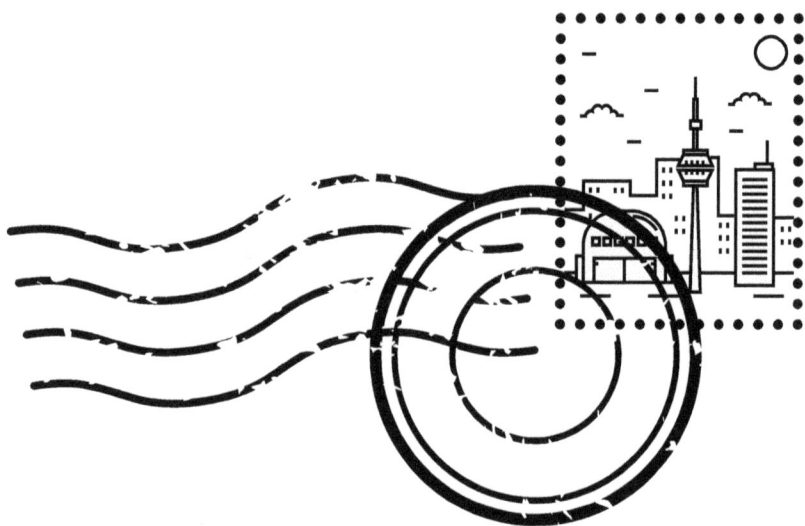

Safety Is a Love Language

Begin with safety, but not the kind built from fear. This is not panic. This is clarity. This is preparation.

Meet in public. Tell someone where you're going. Keep your phone charged. Leave when your gut tightens, and your body hums with a quiet no. You don't owe anyone comfort at the expense of your own peace. You don't need a detailed reason to walk away. "No" is a full sentence, isn't it?

You're allowed to listen to your intuition like it's earned a seat at the table—because it has.

Many of us were taught to be nice before we were taught to be safe. We learned to explain away our unease, to second-guess the voice inside that says something isn't right. We were encouraged to give people the benefit of the doubt while ignoring the benefit of our own survival.

Let me be clear: you are not overreacting. You are not rude for choosing yourself. You don't need a reason to leave a date, a chat, or a conversation that has started to bruise.

Some men won't raise their voice. They will compliment your taste, ask about your dreams, learn your patterns. Then echo them back until you mistake reflection for resonance. He might tell you you're different before he knows your favorite song. He could say that he's never felt this way before—on the second date. He may race forward and call it passion. But that kind of speed only induces pressure (no, thanks, am I right?). It's urgency masquerading as care. You confuse it with depth. But this way of being isn't connection—it's choreography.

And then, one morning, he stops texting. You ask yourself if you dreamed it all. You didn't. You were just moving too fast to catch the signs.

27

So we slow down. We meet in daylight. We keep friends informed. We stay alert, not anxious. We remember that love, when real, doesn't demand we abandon ourselves. Love expands. It does not erase.

You're Not a Supporting Character

Even when a date goes well—when it's kind, when it makes you laugh—you still deserve to be seen beyond what you offer. You are not a therapist. Not a muse. Not a supporting character in someone else's comeback story. You are your own main character, and you don't have to make anyone else's healing your responsibility.

Let dating be messy. Let it be a little weird (quirky isn't a bad thing… and it's fun to say). Let it have space for nervous laughter, for mismatched timing, for stories you'll tell your friends later over drinks and fries. Not every encounter is meant to lead somewhere permanent. Some are brief. Some are blurry. Some are beautiful and then gone. That's okay. You're not a failure for wanting more than a moment—but also not demanding every moment turn into more.

Let go of the idea that there's a finish line. Let go of the idea that being chosen is the prize. The real gift is staying rooted while the wind of someone else's affection blows near. You do not need to grip. You do not need to plead. You do not need to stay if it's good but not right.

You can leave when your heart is still open. You can end something kindly. You can say, "Thank you," and still walk away.

That is power. That is self-trust. That is what it looks like to belong to yourself.

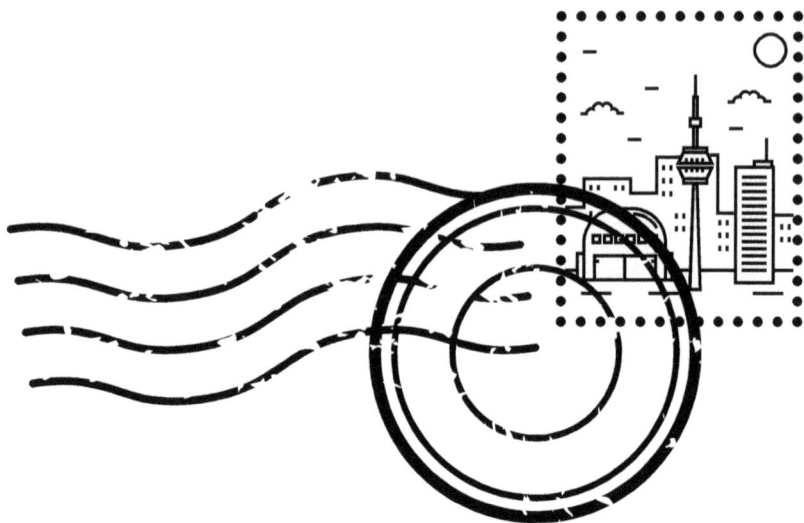

For the Ones Reading
Closely

This book won't hand you the perfect script. It won't prevent every mistake or heartbreak. But it will walk with you. It'll hold your hand. Through quiet mornings when you wonder if you're too much. Through awkward coffee dates. Through long nights texting a friend to ask, "Was it weird when he said that?"

In these pages, I've remembered myself more times than I've lost her. I've met men who mistook my openness for emptiness. I've learned from cultures that hold dating as taboo, dangerous, or impossible for women. To the women who've had to sneak glances, who can't meet in cafes or speak openly—I see you. Love, for you, may live in hope more than habit. And still, your experience matters. You deserve safety, privacy, choice.

To the women reading this: You are not too intense. You are not difficult. You are not hard to love. You are paying attention. And that's brave.

To the men reading this: Thank you for being here. This isn't a code to crack. This is an invitation. Read with care. Let it change the way you listen, the way you show up.

To non-binary and gender-diverse readers: You are welcome here. This story starts in one voice, but it belongs to more than one body. Love doesn't have a fixed shape. Neither does truth.

This book doesn't end with a wedding. There is no magic password to being chosen. But there is something honest waiting here: the joy of knowing yourself so well that even when love shows up, you don't disappear.

You can leave good dates. You can reject lovely people. You can say no after "yes" stops feeling safe. That's allowed. That's adult. That's sovereign.

You are not a problem to solve. You are a person to honor.

So if you're here to fall in love, beautiful. If you're here to stand taller in your own skin, even better.

Put on the earrings that make you feel powerful. Drink water. Tell someone where you're going. Say your own name out loud until it sounds like home.

Let's go.

Date 1
Ryan: The Celtic Experiment

Sometimes the right person comes too early—not to stay, but to teach you how to stay for yourself.

Ryan showed me what love looks like when it arrives wearing quiet courage and puts you first—before pride, before fear, before need. He was the kind of man who didn't chase romance like a prize but treated it like a responsibility. Loving him made me realize: the kind of devotion I admired in others, I had to learn to offer to myself.

1 - Ryan:

Because I am eclectic, open-minded, and emotionally agile, people often assume I go for the stereotypical "alpha male" type. You know, tall, tattooed, rugged—the kind of man who could bench press your car and carry you over his shoulder while quoting Marcus Aurelius.

Sometimes that assumption isn't completely wrong.

There's something permissive, almost experimental, about choosing someone like that. It's like testing a stereotype in a controlled environment: What happens when a strong woman chooses a strong man who looks like a walking plot twist?

When Ryan walked into my life—tall, bald, thick-shouldered, with full-sleeve tattoos and a red-nosed pit bull — he felt like a social experiment in motion. He looked exactly like the kind of guy people imagined me with. He even had a slight limp, like a Viking who survived a shipwreck and came out stronger. He wasn't trying to impress anyone. He was the impression.

I was intrigued.

He was also German-Scottish, with a practical Celtic sense of humor and a deep voice that made mundane things like grocery lists sound like war chants. He didn't text much, but when he did, it was direct and oddly poetic, in a "me Tarzan, you Jane with a master's degree" kind of way.

Our first date felt like a rom-com: him in black jeans and boots, me in a coat I had no business wearing inside. We met in a neutral place—downtown, by a dog park—and he introduced me to his dog before introducing himself. Priorities, apparently.

Full disclosure: I come from a mixed background. My father is Black and deeply old-fashioned. Tattoos, in his worldview, were more than just ink. They were statements—loud ones. Growing up, I assumed body art was something he would never tolerate in a potential son-in-law. But after Ryan, and many conversations later, I found out otherwise.

I once asked him what he thought of tattoos, preparing myself for the speech I was sure would come. Instead, he surprised me.

"If you were happy, I'd be happy," he said. "What matters is who the person is." Then he smirked. "Besides, it's too late now, right?"

And just like that, my dad dropped a truth bomb wrapped in casual charm. The real lesson? Sometimes we inherit limits we never challenge—until someone with full sleeves and a rescue pit bull makes us question them.

But back to Ryan.

He was older—seven years, to be exact. In Brazil, that kind of age gap is barely worth noting. Here in Canada, it raised eyebrows. Age difference is coded differently in every culture. In North America, seven years is seen as a "power imbalance" potential. In Brazil? It's practically normal. I didn't care about the number—I cared about how we made each other feel.

And he made me feel... curious. There was something heavy behind his eyes, like he was always carrying something just out of view. His tattoos were intense—not artistic, but angry. Guns, skulls, violent symbols, things that made you wonder what kind of story was behind all that ink.

Still, I pushed forward. I wasn't there to judge. I was there to learn—about him, about myself, about the things that made us who we are.

We went on a few dates. He was respectful and kind in a rough-a-round-the-edges way. He'd pick quiet places. He didn't drink. He listened carefully and spoke softly, which felt almost eerie coming from someone who looked like a nightclub bouncer.

One night, after a warm dinner and a slow walk, he dropped it. "I have chronic kidney failure," he said. "I'm waiting for a transplant."

I was stunned. Not because he was sick—people get sick. But because of what he said next. "You deserve better than me. You're just starting your life. I'm lucky to have met you. But keeping you would be bad karma."

I blinked. It was a punch in the gut. Nobody had ever broken up with me before. Especially not like this—with kindness and a clear boundary. I wasn't sure whether to feel angry or sad. It wasn't rejection in the traditional sense. It was something heavier—like being exiled for my own good.

He told me I was too radiant for his darkness. That loving me would make him feel guilty. He wanted me to find someone who could offer more than hospital visits and waiting lists. Then he blocked me. Just like that. Disappeared. He didn't ghost me; he respectfully vanished like a knight who walks himself into exile before the story ends.

And that was the most disorienting part—I didn't get a say. I didn't get to process, to rage, to stay in the story. He closed the book without warning.

I remember sitting on my couch afterward, staring at the blank chat screen and thinking: Am I devastated… or relieved?

The truth is, I'd always thought breakups were a kind of relief—a painful but necessary evolution. This one was different. It felt like being protected and violated at the same time. Like he'd saved me from something I didn't know I needed saving from, and also robbed me of the right to decide.

I processed it quickly. Maybe too quickly. Part of me wanted to respect his choice. Another part of me just didn't know where to place the sadness.

But my mind, ever the resilient scientist of emotion, went into analysis mode: If I found someone so intriguing so quickly… surely there are more good ones out there.

Spoiler alert: I wasn't wrong.

Tip from this date: Don't jinx yourself by assuming the first good one is the good one. The universe loves an ego check.

What I learned from Ryan was that appearances deceive, pain hides in plain sight, and sometimes love isn't about who stays but who steps away with grace.

He taught me that people come into your life to awaken parts of yourself you didn't even know were asleep. I didn't fall in love with Ryan. But I fell into something—a moment, a crack in my own certainty, a glimpse of what strength looks like in silence.

And that was enough.

Onward.

Cultural Glimpse - The Celtic

In Celtic culture, strength is stitched with sorrow. The men carry both myth and mud—warrior bones wrapped in wool and restraint. Ryan didn't need many words. His silence held the weight of entire bloodlines. Even his limp felt like legacy.

Date 2
Rohan: Bon Jovi Land

Not every love story needs a sequel—some just need a great soundtrack and a sunset.

Rohan reminded me that a single weekend can hold a lifetime's worth of joy. He taught me how to savor connection for what it is, not what it could become. Some dates are like movies: full of charm, color, and perfect endings that don't ask for more. With him, I learned to live in the scene—no pause, no fast forward. Just play: "Its My life."

2 - Rohan:

I learned English because of Jon Bon Jovi.
Not for school. Not for a job.
I wanted to feel the music.

I remember pressing "play" on my cheap stereo and trying to mimic every line. I didn't know what he was saying, but I knew what he meant. There was something raw in his voice—something about heartbreak, hope, defiance.

I wanted to understand it all. Not just translate it—feel it. So, I learned word by word, song by song. Somewhere between "Always" and "Keep the Faith," I carved out a dream I didn't know I was building: A life shaped by language, emotion, and the belief that music—and love—are worth chasing.

So yes, it's fair to say this whole book probably started with Bon Jovi. That's why, when I matched with Rohan—a soft-eyed, gentle-voiced man from New Jersey—I laughed out loud.

Bon Jovi Land.

Could this be fate? A full-circle moment wrapped in denim and destiny? Rohan wasn't a rockstar, but he had a quiet magnetism. He was kind. The kind of kind you don't expect anymore. He listened. He laughed easily. He texted like a grown-up. For our first date, he suggested something wild: Ice skating.

I had never skated before. Not once. I had no idea what I was doing.

I told him I'd probably break a hip or an ego, but he just laughed and said, "Perfect. I'll bring bubble wrap."

There I was, clinging to a cold rail at Nathan Phillips Square, legs wobbling like a baby deer in heels, while he skated backwards in slow circles around me like some annoyingly graceful Canadian flamingo.

"Are you even human?" I yelled.

He shrugged, grinning. "This is Jersey talent, baby."

I hated how good he was at it. But I loved how he didn't make fun of me when I clutched his jacket with full panic in my eyes.

He didn't rush me. He didn't mock my fear. He made jokes, light ones, the kind that made you feel safe instead of small.

"You're doing great," he said once, as I slid half a meter on my own before crashing into him.

"That counts as Olympic-level progress."

We skated for less than an hour, but it felt like the whole date was held in that delicate space between terror and laughter.

When it ended, he walked me back to the subway, gave me a hug that felt like warm corduroy, and said, "I think you're braver than you realize."

Then he left. No grand goodbye. No dramatic exit. Just a sweet wave and a man walking home in the cold. I never saw him again. And honestly? That was okay. Some people aren't meant to stay.

Some are just meant to show up, hold your hand when you're scared, and remind you that you can let go of the rail.

Rohan didn't rock my world. He steadied it for an afternoon. And Bon Jovi? He didn't just teach me English. He taught me how to believe in moments like that.

Cultural Glimpse - The American

In the U.S., dreams are taught before tenderness. Many men are raised to fix, to fight, to finish what hurts. But Rohan was from New Jersey—the land of Aerosmith ache and Bon Jovi heart. He didn't just walk me home. He walked me back to something gentle.

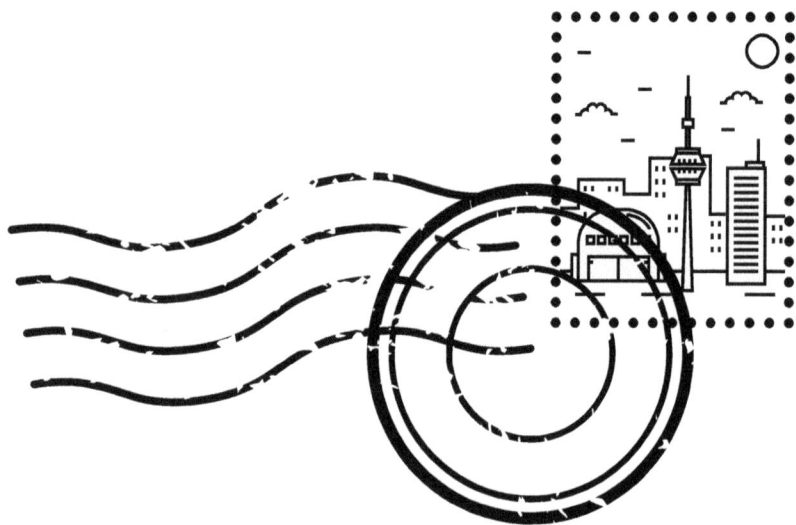

Date 3
Allan: The Croatian Spectrum

Some loyalties are beautiful from afar—and suffocating up close.

We used to meet near St. Lawrence Market, where the old-world charm feels both inviting and unchanging. It suited Allan. There was something solid about him—family-first, community-rooted, Balkan-proud. But in that pride, I found a pressure. He taught me the beauty of loyalty, yes—but also where it ends and where I begin. There's a fine line between belonging and disappearing.

And I realized I didn't want to walk it quite so close.

3 – Allan:

After Ryan and Rohan, I found myself branching out to the other end of the cultural spectrum.

If online dating had taught me anything, it was that curiosity is far more useful than having a "type." And honestly, I had also begun to embrace what made me... well, exotic.

Being "exotic" was a complicated compliment. It could sound as enticing as forbidden candy, or as borderline-offensive as an outdated law. I took it as I chose, and mostly — I chose to laugh. I never felt obligated to fit into a box that someone else needed to label.

People could define. I would live.

So I began scrolling through profiles like an HR consultant sifting through half-qualified candidates. Swipe. Swipe. Swipe.

One morning, it hit me: Is there even a procedure manual for this? No roadmap, no checklist. Just my instincts, my humor, my curiosity—the firefighter in me knowing that in a multicultural society like this one, mingling should be a sport, not a disease.

I decided, right then, that I would simply learn. Meet people, enjoy the ride, and trust that clarity would come in its own time.

That Monday morning, Allan's message appeared. Tall, slightly older (four years, which was perfect), blond turning a little bald, with piercing blue eyes—he looked like the father of every doll from a Brazilian girl's childhood. Exactly the kind of face that generations of Brazilian mothers dreamed their daughters would marry.

He was Serbian-Croatian by background — born and raised here, but still wrapped in the cultural codes of a tight-knit community.

In Croatian families, loyalty to your blood, your parents, and your traditions is sacred. Respect isn't optional. Family isn't a chapter — it's the whole book. And Allan lived that deeply.

He spoke of his mother often — an older German-Serbian woman, stern but wise — and not once with resentment. He admired and respected her in a way I rarely saw in men our age — not in words alone, but in small, consistent glimpses of love.

It was... charming—but only at first, soon, I started to notice something else underneath it all: the pressure.

Family wasn't simply a beautiful tradition for Allan—it was also a weight he carried around, like an invisible second skin. Every story, every plan, every dream he spoke of seemed to come with a background chorus: "Would my family approve?" "Would this fit the mold?" "Would I be seen as a good son?"

At first, it was subtle—almost sweet. But over time, it felt heavy. A constant negotiation between what he might want and what they might expect.

This wasn't a shock to me. In many immigrant cultures, family pressure is the background music of life. But with Allan, it was so intertwined into his choices, his thinking, even his laughter—it made me worry. How much room was left for him inside his own story? How much room would there ever be for me?

We texted and exchanged voice notes for weeks. His audios made me laugh until my stomach hurt—he could imitate half a dozen voices perfectly. He wasn't just smart (a data analyst, naturally), he was hilarious in that dry, unexpected way that creeps up on you when you least expect it.

I wasn't in a hurry. I had learned my lesson by now: let conversations unfold, let the curiosity breathe.

When we finally met in person, the connection was there—but so was that undercurrent of tension. Excitement... and a faint feeling of inadequacy. I didn't recognize it at first.

I had always walked into dates feeling solid, composed. But with Allan, I suddenly felt... evaluated. Analyzed. He was kind, polite, even funny in person. But it felt like he was running invisible equations behind his bright blue eyes. Calculating compatibility. Assessing risk. Measuring ROI.

I understood it, professionally. He worked with data all day—precision was his survival skill. But romantically? It drained something out of the magic. Dating, after all, isn't math. It's alchemy.

We didn't crash and burn. There were no fights, no tears, no dramatic "last texts." Just a slow, respectful fade-out. It was mutual.

We said our goodbyes, thanked each other for the time, and gently stepped back into our lives. No blocking. No ghosting. Just a silent, peaceful agreement that this—whatever this had been—had run its course.

For me, it was an unexpected victory. I was learning to release my expectations. I didn't have to "win" every encounter. Not every connection needed to be forever to be worth it. Sometimes, what it is all it needs to be. And that, I realized, was a form of emotional fluency I had fought hard to earn.

In Croatia, there's a saying: "Bolje spriječiti nego liječiti." In English, that translates to, "Better to prevent than to cure."

Maybe that's what Allan and I both did—we spared each other the wrong kind of heartbreak before it could grow roots.

In that simple, quiet way... it was still a beautiful success.

Cultural Glimpse - The Balkan

In the Balkans, loyalty is a religion, and family is law. Men are carved by history—strong, stoic, sometimes sealed shut. Allan spoke in gestures more than truths, in pride more than presence. But under the spectrum of silence, I saw a man trying to breathe between borders.

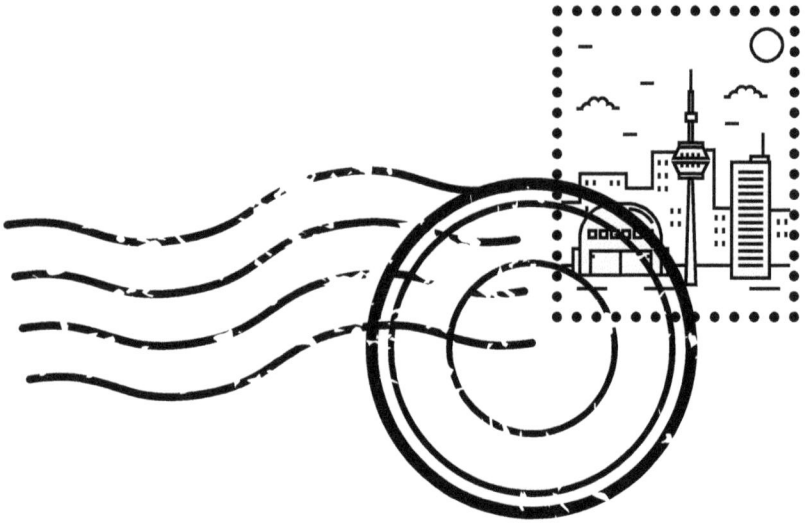

Date 4
Casey: A Lesson in Sensuality and Vietnamese Culture

What if femininity isn't something we perform, but something we remember?

We met near Spadina, where Chinatown gives way to Kensington, and the streets smell like incense and deep-fried sweetness. Casey never asked me to be soft—but somehow, I softened. Not in the way magazines sell it. In the way chopsticks hold things delicately without breaking them. With him, I realized I didn't even like what the world had labeled feminine in me. I wasn't delicate. I was delicious. And femininity? Maybe it's not pink and polite. Maybe it's just presence.

4 - Casey:

When Casey first messaged me, I was surprised.

Sure, Brazil has one of the largest Japanese communities outside of Japan, but I'd never really considered Asian men as "my type." I mean, there was Carlos from high school—of Japanese descent—who tried to date me in Grade 7. But let's just say, he wasn't exactly my Romeo.

So, when Casey slid into my inbox, it felt like new territory.

I was excited. Maybe it was time to open my mind.

Casey was older, highly educated, and an absolute expert in the art of sensual conversation—not in a "let's make out" kind of way, but in how he made everything sound alive. We started talking about food—Vietnamese food, specifically—and suddenly, I was hooked.

With Casey, food wasn't just nourishment. It was an experience. He described dishes like they were stories. The crunch of spring rolls, the silkiness of pho broth, the fragrant chaos of herbs and spices—he made you feel the meal before you even saw it.

Talking to him felt like tasting the world. Vietnamese food, he explained, was all about balance. Not just on the plate but in life. Sweet, salty, sour. Hot, cold, fresh, fermented. Everything in its place. Every flavor had a job to do.

I'd never thought about food that way before. But the more he spoke, the more it resonated—he was speaking to something deeper than food: presence. The way Vietnamese culture slows down for meals. The way a shared table becomes a sacred ritual. Even the way chopsticks hold a piece of fish is part of the experience.

We talked for hours. And then there were the stories. One day, he started teaching me about coconuts. Yes—coconuts. I always thought coconuts were as Brazilian as samba and beach soccer. But Casey told me they're travelers. Oceanic nomads. They float across seas, land on distant shores, and root themselves in unfamiliar soil.

It was poetic — like him.

In those conversations, I wasn't just learning about Vietnamese cuisine—I was learning how to be curious again. How to listen with more than just my ears. How to see the world through someone else's senses.

But when we finally met in person... something shifted. He wasn't what I had pictured. He was softer, almost feminine in a way that threw me off. It wasn't a flaw—just different. And different can be disorienting when you've built up chemistry in the safety of text and voice notes.

Our connection had been electric online—funny, flirty, thoughtful. But in person, the spark was dimmer. There was no drama, no ghosting—just a slow, natural fade.

Eventually, we slipped into friendship. It was swift, easy, and strangely comforting—like the relationship had simply found its true form. We stopped trying to make it romantic, and in doing so, made space for something even more valuable.

We kept talking. He kept teaching.

And I kept learning—about food, about culture, about the simple joys of discovery. I realized something: Not every meaningful connection is meant to last. Not every lesson needs a love story.

Casey taught me to taste life. To savor it with my entire being. The way he spoke about balance stayed with me.

The coconut's journey across oceans became a quiet metaphor for migration, identity, and even love. Everything about our conversations reminded me that the world is bigger, richer, more sensual than I'd allowed myself to notice.

Even though we didn't last as lovers, I'm grateful. Because sometimes, the deepest impressions are left not by people who stay, but by those who show you a part of the world—and yourself—you hadn't met yet.

With Casey, I learned that sensuality isn't always about romance. Sometimes it's about being fully alive in the moment and honoring every flavor life gives you.

Cultural Glimpse - The Vietnamese

In Vietnam, love is often served in bowls, not in promises. Scent, texture, patience—everything is offered slowly, with care. Casey didn't express his feelings with words. He prepared them. With him, sensuality wasn't sexual—it was sacred, simmered, and shared.

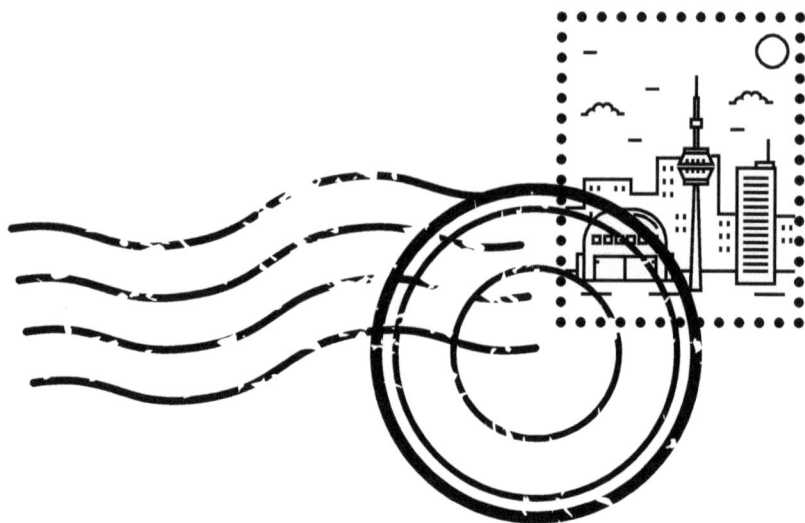

Date 5
Jason: Mr. Maple Leaf

There's a kind of man who'll kill you with kindness. Not the aggressive kind. The quiet, agreeable, ever-helpful kind. The kind who'll say, "No worries," while gently erasing your boundaries one polite gesture at a time. Jason was that kind of man.

He held doors, remembered anniversaries, listened without interrupting. He showed up, every time. And yet, there was a point where I stopped showing up for myself—because it was easier to go along than to confront the aching silence between his sweetness and my unmet needs.

This chapter taught me that niceness isn't the same as presence. That steadiness can feel like safety... until it starts to feel like sedation. And that a man doesn't have to raise his voice to make you doubt yours. Jason was lovely. But sometimes lovely isn't enough.

5 - Jason:

Jason was cute. If I had to draw a stereotypical Canadian man, it would be Jason. Tall, fair-skinned, clean-shaven, polite to a fault, with a baseball cap seemingly fused to his head—and a heart so decent you could frame it.

He was the kind of guy you could picture building a deck, raising two blonde kids, and cheering at hockey games with. If that's what you want, of course.

By Brazilian standards, Canadians are heaven-sent husbands. Reliable, loyal, and generally allergic to cheating. Especially White Canadians from English-speaking families—if you cheat here, you're not just dumped; you're socially crucified. Gender doesn't matter. Shame is distributed democratically.

Jason worked as an air traffic controller—so, naturally, control was his entire brand. Everything about him screamed: "I have a plan. I have a backup plan. And I have a laminated emergency backup for the backup."

I immigrated to Canada as a young adult. I didn't grow up soaking in the culture—I had to study it.

To become a citizen, you take a test that includes everything from Indigenous treaties to the significance of curling. Very helpful for ceremonies. Completely useless on Tinder.

Jason was curious about me. I could see it in his eyes—that look people give mangos when they first discover the fruit section in an international grocery store. He thought I was exotic. But I was happy to show him that exotic didn't mean strange. It meant fabulous.

On our first date, he basically handed me a résumé. Salary, job stability, number of vacation days, projected retirement plan. I could tell it was a speech he had rehearsed—polished like a fire extinguisher under the bed. Just in case.

At first, I was baffled. Where was the improvisation? The poetry? The delightful chaos of not knowing what comes next? In Brazil, dating is samba—spontaneous, unpredictable, full of rhythm. In Canada, dating is curling—strategic, deliberate, and everyone wears a helmet just in case. I didn't know people here planned entire years of vacation ahead of time. What about possibilities? What if you woke up and wanted to chase the Northern Lights instead of lying on a Cancun beach?

Jason's version of romance came with spreadsheets. Even his heritage was mapped—six generations deep. He was a walking Ancestry.com.

Meanwhile, I barely know my blood type. (And honestly, I only know that because I was a firefighter.)

He loved baseball and the Monarchy. Yes—the British Monarchy. He could talk about Prince Harry with a mix of sarcasm and reverence I'd never heard before. "The Monarchy," he said, "is like comfort food—historical continuity without actual power." Somehow, he made me want to believe in crowns again...or at least, consider the idea.

Jason was like poutine: warm, dependable, satisfying if you're craving safety. But if you're not? It can feel heavy. There was a quiet sadness about him, like a fog he'd grown used to living in. Not dramatic, not attention-seeking. Just... there. Polite and silent, like everything else in Canada.

I often wondered if that sadness came from expectations he never questioned. In Brazil, sadness is public. Loud. Colorful. In Canada, sadness is private. Silent. Noble, almost. Even in bed, Jason was surprisingly open-minded. The first time: picture two elephants trying to dance in a crystal shop—chaotic, hilarious, limbs everywhere.

But we were quick learners. We found rhythm. Passionate. Efficient. Royal, even. We dated for a while. Shared Sunday breakfasts. Had in-depth debates about maple syrup ethics and hockey team rivalries. There were sweet moments. Real moments. But eventually, his self-loathing began to dim my fire. Because you can't love someone into believing they deserve joy. No matter how fabulous you are.

We didn't fight. We didn't ghost. We just drifted—like two good people who belonged to different seasons. Jason was a beautiful frozen lake. I was a tropical storm. And that's okay.

Sometimes love doesn't mean fixing or forcing. It's more about recognizing when to let go—with grace, with warmth, with gratitude.

I think of Jason fondly. I hope he found someone who sees the poetry in his plans. Someone who dances to his carefully composed rhythm.

My time with Jason helped me learn that planning is a beautiful thing. But some of the best things in life happen when you throw the map out the window. Even poutine tastes better when you improvise the toppings.

Cultural Glimpse - The Canadian

In Canada, kindness is currency, and restraint is a kind of reverence. Men like Jason don't rush—they reliably arrive. He was maple syrup in winter: slow, steady, and sweet once you let him thaw. Not a spark—but a hearth. Not drama—but devotion.

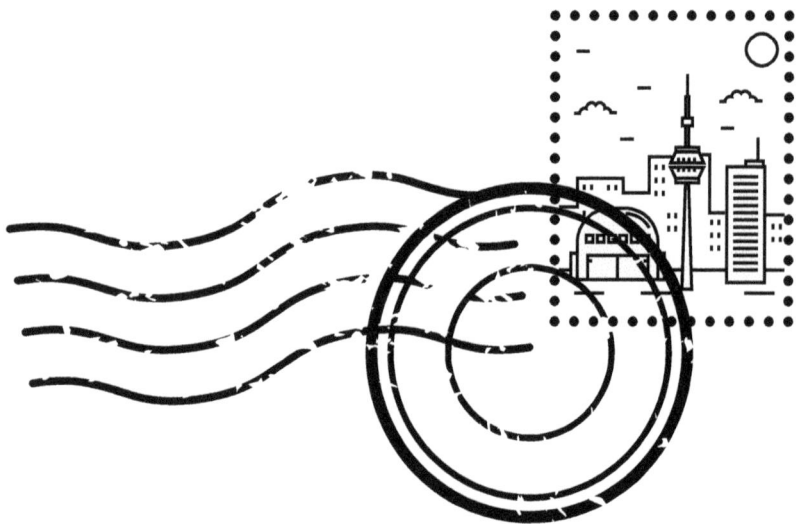

Date 6
Alex: A Mediterranean Lesson in Freedom

Before Alex, I thought every man was either a test or a trap. After Alex, I started to see them as teachers.

He didn't seduce me. He didn't chase me. He just was—open, honest, already loved, already loving. And somehow, that made space for me to ask a different kind of question. This wasn't a love story. It was a re-education.

In trust. In freedom. In the possibility that choosing differently didn't make me wrong—just braver.

6 - Alex:

Alex wasn't the kind of man you just met. You noticed him. Tanned skin that looked straight out of a Sicilian postcard. Thick black hair. Striking green eyes. An audio engineer by day, Brazilian jiu-jitsu black belt by hobby — brains, beauty, and a smile that could undo your whole day. In Brazil, we'd call him a classic molha calcinha—the kind of man who made women lose their balance without even trying.

So, when his message landed in my inbox, I genuinely thought it was a scam. Handsome, articulate, confident without being cocky — where was the catch? I was waiting for the crypto pitch. Or some vague "business opportunity." But none came.

Instead, Alex introduced himself like a polished professional. Clear. Warm. Slightly formal. It felt less like flirting and more like onboarding for a promising new position. I found it hilarious... and charming. We talked. He was steady, curious, and surprisingly respectful. And then, as casually as someone might mention a favorite soccer team, he dropped it: "By the way, I'm in an open marriage."

I blinked at the screen. Once. Twice. I grew up in Brazil—land of sunshine, samba, and famously flexible affection—but still, we're weirdly colonial when it comes to relationships.

Cheating? Common. Consensual non-monogamy? That was scandalous. My first reaction was pure Catholic-school scandal: "Meu Deus." My second was worse: judgment.

It took a few days to get over myself enough to even respond. When I did, it wasn't to accuse—it was to ask. Alex, to his credit, answered every question without a hint of defensiveness. He told me he and his wife had started out traditional. Fell in love, built their life together. But over time, they realized love didn't have to be a cage—and desire wasn't betrayal. So, they talked. They built rules. They carved out a structure rooted not in fear, but in freedom.

"Jealousy isn't proof of love," he said. "It's proof of fear. You can feel it. You just don't have to obey it."

They didn't control each other. They chose each other—again and again—even with the freedom not to.

Something inside me cracked open. I'd never questioned monogamy—not really. It was the default. The ideal. The right way to love. But now I started seeing all the hairline fractures in that perfect picture.

How many couples did I know who were monogamous in form, but emotionally miserable? How many built their loyalty on fear, routine, or guilt?

Alex wasn't trying to convert me. He wasn't selling anything. He was just living proof that love could look different—and still be beautiful. Ethical. Joyful. Grown.

The fact that he looked like Antonio Banderas with a side of Colin Farrell didn't exactly hurt his case. All salt and pepper, sly glances, and a voice you could sip like red wine.

We kept talking. Laughing. Trading stories. Sharing our cultural codes like secret recipes. But I didn't stay. Not because of him. Not because of polyamory. Because of me.

At that moment in my life, I wasn't ready. The idea of loving more than one person with clarity, grace, and constant communication? Beautiful. But overwhelming.

I admired the freedom he lived. I just wasn't fluent in that language. Not yet. And that was okay.

What Alex gave me wasn't a new relationship. It was a new lens.

There are as many ways to love as there are hearts to hold it. Monogamy can be sacred. So can polyamory. The model doesn't matter. The intention does.

Cultural Note: Polyamory is often misunderstood. At its best, it's not chaos—it's choreography. A commitment to honesty, autonomy, empathy, and emotional fluency. It's not for everyone. But neither is monogamy. One isn't more evolved. One isn't more moral. They're just different ways to navigate the wild ocean of human connection.

If there's one truth I took from Alex, it's this: Love isn't one-size-fits-s-all. It's a living, breathing force—and you are allowed to shape it in a way that makes you feel free.

Maybe you'll choose one partner. Maybe you'll love two. Maybe your model will change. That's not failure. That's growth. If you listen closely to your own heart, you'll find love that fits like a second skin. And that's the beginning of a whole new map.

Cultural Glimpse - The Mediterranean

In Italy and Greece, love is loud, and sex is fluent. Pleasure is not taboo—it is taught, inherited, expected. But Alex turned the flame inward: freedom over possession, truth over tradition. He didn't just speak of love. He redefined its terms.

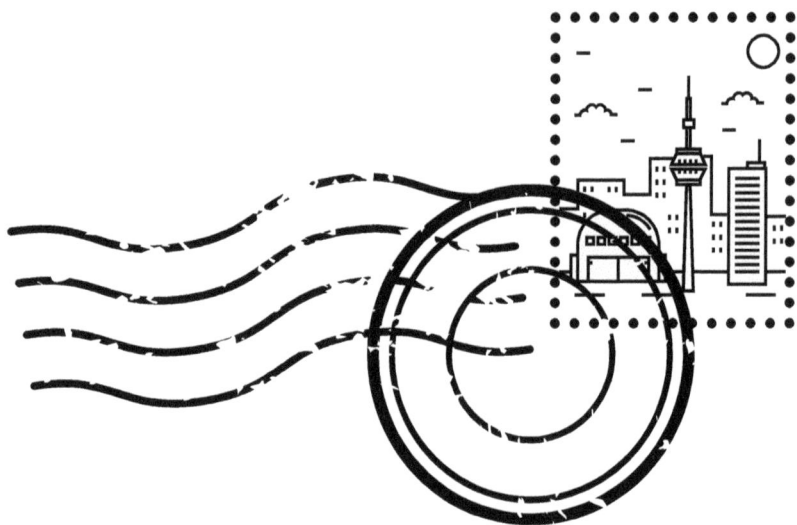

Date 7
Sean: The Irish with a Broken Heart

There are parts of Toronto that feel like confessionals—quiet corners near St. Michael's Cathedral, the hushed pews of Our Lady of Sorrows, or even just a Sunday streetcar ride down Queen West when the city is still waking up. That's where Sean lived—in those soft, sacred silences that made you feel safe but not quite seen.

With him, I had the passport. I had the paperwork. But I still felt like a foreigner in his world. Two citizens of heaven, maybe—but with very different definitions of grace.

This was the chapter where I learned: shared faith isn't the same as shared language. And sometimes, even the gentlest men can make you feel like a guest in your own country.

7 - Sean:

Sean was a landscaper. And a Catholic. Which shouldn't have surprised me—and yet it did. Maybe I'm not as smart as I think I am. Or maybe I'm just highly impressionable. Probably both. I was raised Catholic too—baptized in one of the last Catholic-Orthodox churches in the Americas. My certificate looks like a rare diplomatic document, recognized by both branches of the faith. To me, that's dual citizenship in heaven. At least, that's the joke I like to make.

But Catholicism in Brazil is different. It's looser. Lighter. More infused with music, dance, and syncretism than shame or sin. People cross themselves before dancing samba, drink caipirinhas after mass, and casually merge Christianity with indigenous and African spiritual beliefs. It's faith, but with rhythm.

Sean's Catholicism, however, was rooted in ritual. His faith was quiet, structured, reverent—more British than Brazilian. It felt less like a connection to the divine and more like a lifelong performance review with God as your silent supervisor.

And Sean was just like his religion: soft-spoken, loyal, a little sad. He had blue-collar hands, kind eyes, and an Irish accent so thick it felt like a second language. Sometimes, I had to ask him to repeat himself. At first, he thought I was teasing. But when he realized I was laughing with him—not at him—a sweet, shy smile replaced his suspicion.

But here's the thing about Sean that truly stunned me: He was a father. Not biologically. Not at first legally. But fully, completely, in every way that mattered. His former partner had gotten pregnant after their relationship began. The biological father had disappeared before the baby was born. Sean stayed. He raised the child from day one.

Eventually, he became her legal father under Canadian law—not because he had to, but because he chose to. That act alone undid me.

In Brazil, where many men dodge even their own biological responsibilities, meeting someone who chose fatherhood with that kind of integrity felt revolutionary. But it also made me realize something I hadn't considered before—something that changed how I viewed Sean and my own role in the relationship.

In Canada, if you live with someone who has a child, you can become legally responsible, too. You don't have to marry them. You don't even have to adopt the child. You just have to be there long enough, love deeply enough, and suddenly, the law sees you as a "de facto" parent. That means if you separate, you could be responsible for child support. It's a legal system built to protect children from instability, which is noble in theory. But when you're dating, just dating—especially as a woman—that's a terrifying amount of invisible weight.

I hadn't met Sean's daughter, and we weren't even living together. But I couldn't ignore the shadow she cast over every conversation, every plan, every moment of intimacy.

She was always present—gently, respectfully—in the background. In the way he structured his week. In the way he answered his phone. In the way he talked about love: not as a fire, but as a responsibility. Dating someone with a child, I learned, isn't simply adjusting to nap schedules or avoiding loud restaurants. It means stepping into a story that's already in motion.

You don't get to be the main character. You don't even get to be in the prologue. You're joining halfway through, with no control over the script. There's beauty in that—and there's grief. Even if things don't work out, even if you never meet the child, you still carry the weight of that potential future. A future you were almost part of. And that almost can feel like a quiet loss no one talks about.

Sean was kind, steady, emotionally restrained. He loved deeply, but quietly. And I often felt like my joy—my spontaneity, my loud Brazilian laughter—made him uncomfortable. Not because he didn't like it, but because it stirred something in him that had long been buried. He was a man of silence. A man of service. He knew how to give, but not how to be seen.

He once told me: "If I wasn't in church every Sunday, I'd be in a bar."

His faith saved him from self-destruction. But it didn't necessarily bring him peace. There was a sadness in him, one he carried like an invisible coat. It wasn't loud. It was noble. Quiet. Almost sacred. And I couldn't fix it.

We didn't break up. We just drifted. Two good people, walking in different emotional climates. Sean needed a partner who could offer silence, softness, and predictability. I was a storm. A wildfire. The wrong kind of weather. But I don't regret him.

Sean taught me what responsible love looks like. What devotion means when no one is watching. He reminded me that fatherhood is about presence, not genetics—and that real masculinity isn't loud, but steadfast. He also taught me to look at the legal side of love. That caring for someone with a child isn't just emotional—it's contractual. And that entering someone's life when they come as a package deal means confronting your own limits.

What are you ready for? What are you responsible for—even when it's unspoken? That's not romantic. But it's real.

Final Snapshot: A rosary swaying from the rearview mirror. A lunchbox in the passenger seat. A quiet man choosing love, one unseen act at a time.

Cultural Glimpse - The Irish

In Irish Catholic homes, silence is devotion and duty is love's disguise. Emotion runs deep but speaks in whispers, through rosaries and restraint. Sean carried sorrow like a second skin—but he still showed up. His tenderness wasn't loud. It was liturgical.

Date 8
Jace: The Canadian Soulander

There's a hush in the Don Valley—the kind of hush that feels older than the city itself. That's where I met The Soulander. But that's not the name he gave me. It's the name I gave him. In honor of the ones who came before us. The ones who named everything not by how they looked, but by how they felt. I named him in my own head and heart, (felt like called by my own indigenous ancestors) the way our people name: by the way he feels.

Jace felt like soul. Like land. Like memory buried under pavement and still breathing. He didn't speak much, but when he did, it was like listening to bark separate from a tree—slow, necessary, true.

This was the chapter where I remembered that not all love stories are loud. That some men arrive not to ignite passion, but to return you to yourself. That silence can be a language. And that connection, when rooted in lineage, doesn't need to bloom to mean something sacred.

8 - Jace:

I met Jace while studying Medical Record Keeping at the University of Toronto.

It was a messy, hopeful, transitional time in my life—one of those seasons where you're building something real, without yet knowing what shape it will take.

School was chaotic, the city cold, and my daily life a mosaic of dreams, deadlines, and too many winter jackets.

Jace was First Nations—Mohawk, from the Haudenosaunee Confederacy. Somehow, even after years of living in Canada, this was the first time I was truly seeing the Indigenous peoples of this land.

In Brazil, Indigenous history is treated like a beautiful ghost—referenced, respected, and then immediately buried under 500 years of colonization, genocide, and silence. You grow up knowing there were once people who spoke to the rivers and the stars. But you don't hear their names at dinner. You don't see their faces on banknotes. You just feel the absence.

When I met Jace—or, more accurately, observed him from across our class for weeks—I felt something shift.

He wasn't flashy. He wasn't flirty. He wasn't trying to impress anyone. He simply was. Still. Rooted. Like a cedar tree wearing flannel. He didn't give off any signs. No cocked eyebrow. No charming smirk. He'd just nod politely and go back to his reading. Which, of course, only made me more determined. I mean—did he not know how good his hair looked? The man could've been a shampoo commercial wrapped in cultural wisdom.

One afternoon, I decided to make my move—subtle, elegant, smooth. "Coffee?" I asked, casually.

He looked startled. "Oh... um... I'm busy today. Sorry." He said it so politely, I almost believed he had a dentist appointment with the Creator.

Defeated but not discouraged, I smiled and turned away.

A few minutes later, he walked back over and said, "Rain check?"

Victory. Sort of.

Jace later admitted even asking for a rain check was out of character. That tiny act — invisible to most — felt enormous once you understood who he was. Stoic. Thoughtful. Deliberate. He was the kind of man who spoke only when he meant it. A rare breed in a world of over--sharers and emoji flirts.

We didn't go for coffee, not right away. Instead, we started talking. It began with class topics, then turned into longer conversations about identity, memory, land. He told me he taught Indigenous Studies. I told him I had Indigenous ancestry in Brazil, buried beneath centuries of assimilation, Catholicism, and carnival.

When I shared that, something changed. He looked at me like we were holding the same broken mirror—scattered pieces of culture we were both trying to glue back together. Our connection wasn't romantic. Not in the way most people mean it. But there was something sacred in the space between us.

We once took a walk together through the Don River Valley Park, where he told me there was an installation he wanted to show me — Monsters for Beauty, Permanence and Individuality, by Duane Linklater.

"Is this a date?" I teased.

He smiled while looking straight ahead. "It's... a walk."

Clearly, my flirting radar was set to "subtle" and his was set to "completely unplugged."

Still, we walked. As we approached the sculptures—towering steel forms that resembled hybrid beings, both animal and spirit—I felt something ancient hum in the back of my chest.

"They're inspired by Indigenous forms from museum collections," he said. "Duane's work is about reclaiming our image. We were documented as artifacts... not people."

We stood in silence for a moment, taking them in. "I like that they're a bit awkward," I said. "Not exactly monsters. Not exactly beautiful. Just... honest."

"Like all of us," he said, softly.

It was that kind of moment intimate, without being romantic. Profound, without needing to be explained. In Brazil, Indigenous rituals often hide inside Catholic ones. Like cutting your hair under the crescent moon to strengthen it—a tradition I followed instinctively, never knowing why. Jace helped me remember why. He didn't do it with lectures. He did it with stories. With questions. With presence. He reminded me that heritage isn't something you study. It's something you live.

Later, just to keep things interesting, I learned he was also... a hockey player. I nearly choked. "You?! Hockey?!"

He laughed. "Why not?"

To see this calm, reverent man lace up skates and body-check people into the boards was absurd. And also, somehow, perfect. Healing, he reminded me, isn't just smudging and ceremony. It's joy. It's sweat. It's play. It's letting the body remember, too.

Jace was many things: A scholar, a soul whisperer, a keeper of stories, a defender of silence, and apparently, a winger with a killer slapshot.

He taught me what it means to be strong without performing strength. What it means to honor the past without drowning in it. What it means to carry history without losing joy.

Nothing romantic ever bloomed between us — unless you count my whispered prayers that he'd kiss me at least once (he did not. Soul whisperer, yes. Mind reader, sadly no.)

What we shared left a deeper imprint than many so-called "great loves." Jace reminded me that identity isn't a costume you wear during heritage month. It's a bone memory. It's a call. It's a reclamation.

He was, and remains, a Soulander — a word I made up just for him. His people are the soul of this land. And through him, I realized something essential: A soul never disappears. It just waits — quietly — to be heard.

Cultural Glimpse - The First Nations (Mohawk)

In Haudenosaunee culture, love is not owned—it is offered in balance, like all things. Silence is presence. Land is language. Healing is ancestral. Jace didn't speak loudly. He remembered deeply. He wasn't just a man. He was a signal from the soul.

Date 9
Dani: The Aussie with Two Baby Mamas and Two Stories

There's something about The Junction, a Toronto neighborhood, in summer—warm sawdust in the air, espresso cups clinking, and men in work boots moving like they're late for something meaningful. That's where Dani belonged. Not just the neighborhood, but the feeling of it. Practical. Uncomplicated. Surprisingly charming.

Dani didn't try to impress me. He just... showed up. And maybe, after all the emotional trapeze acts and half-finished heartbreaks, that was the magic. He had kids. Baggage. A past already lived. But he also had presence, and a kind of easy father-energy that made chaos feel cozy.

This was the chapter where I learned that being a "good man" doesn't mean he's the right partner. That you can be steady, sweet, even sexy—and still not fit the life someone else is building. Sometimes, the lesson isn't in the kiss. It's in the calm.

9 - Dani:

Back to my soulmate catalog. Sometimes, it felt like ordering a mail-order groom. You get to pick out exact dimensions and preferences, but what actually shows up at your door? That was the real gamble.

My background, a cocktail of cultures and adaptations, had gifted me an open mind, and my imagination was always at work, envisioning different versions of happiness. I genuinely believe that happiness is a skill you build inside yourself. I'm generally a content person, not because I ignore reality, but because I've realized we pay the same emotional price for pessimism or optimism. I think seeing the bright side is sexy.

Dani had that gift. He could spot a problem coming from a mile away, then fix it with cheerful efficiency, like a laid-back handyman with a sixth sense for leaks. He was born and raised in a suburb outside Melbourne, Australia, with Northern Italian roots that peeked through in his love of food, his strong family ties, and his uncanny ability to make a perfect risotto. He still had that unmistakable Aussie lilt—relaxed vowels, a cheeky "mate" now and then—and a casual, sun-warmed demeanor like he'd just stepped off a surfboard, even in the middle of winter.

Dani was a carpenter by trade, and it suited him. He had a salt-of-the-earth steadiness you often find in people who work with their hands. He was practical, self-reliant, and charming in an easy Aussie way. Think weathered boots, sawdust on his shirt, a tan that never faded, and a grin that made you feel like everything would be okay. He had the body of a man who lifted timber for a living, and the energy of someone who could make furniture or a family with equal care.

Dani had two children from two different women. His first marriage had ended about a decade before I met him, and to my surprise, he and his ex-wife had evolved into genuine friends. I saw it with my own eyes: easy banter, inside jokes, co-parenting that worked better than most actual relationships I'd seen. It was rare. They didn't just raise kids together. They backed each other up in life.

But life, being the cheeky bastard it is, tossed Dani a curveball. A few years post-divorce, while dating someone new, he found himself staring at a positive pregnancy test, which he hadn't expected or planned. She'd decided to go ahead with the pregnancy on her own terms, and Dani, blindsided, was forced into a new chapter he hadn't signed up for.

Still, he did what good men do. He showed up—even when it was messy, when it hurt, or when the arrangement felt more like an ambush than a family plan.

The second co-parenting relationship was nothing like the first. It was tense, bitter, and drained of warmth. He respected her as the mother of his child, but the vibe was transactional at best. Meanwhile, she had chosen to be a stay-at-home mum, indefinitely, and expected Dani to foot the entire bill, which felt increasingly unfair to him as he tried to balance parenting, paying child support, and having anything left over for himself. Still, he never badmouthed her. That was another thing I admired—his quiet dignity.

Physically, he looked like a postcard from coastal Italy: medium build, thick blond hair, golden-hazel eyes, and skin that browned in the sun. But his essence was all Australia. Under his laid-back charm was a complexity, especially when it came to his past relationships.

Dating Dani sometimes felt like joining a committee. It wasn't necessarily a bad thing. It was a bit like trying to find your seat at a table already set. There was the co-parenting group chat. The school event logistics. The unspoken tension when Baby Mama #2 showed up with icy small talk and legal documents in her purse.

Despite my open heart and adaptable nature, I sometimes felt like I had walked into a play already halfway through. There were ghosts of old conversations lingering in every room. I had never pictured myself as a mother, but I hadn't ruled it out either. I was open. But two baby mamas? That was a whole different blueprint and emotional mortgage.

Dani was good. Solid. Kind. A genuinely wonderful father and a deeply decent man. But he was still navigating too many old contracts: emotional, legal, and otherwise.

I realized I didn't just want a good man. I wanted a ready man. Someone whose past wasn't a tornado still circling the house. Someone who had cleaned up the rubble, patched the roof, and was standing on the porch, ready to build something new with me.

Dani had all the tools. But he hadn't finished the teardown yet. There were flashes of potential: lazy mornings filled with laughter, meals cooked together, the way he made my chaotic energy feel seen and settled. He smelled like cedar and clean soap. He hugged with his whole body.

But there was weight there. I was done with projects. I wasn't a renovation. I was a blueprint. Dani was a truly good man. But he wasn't my man—not because he failed. I finally learned what it felt like to choose myself and not just the possibility of love.

Cultural Glimpse - The Aussie

In Australia, men build before they speak. Humor is armor, and fatherhood often comes before readiness. Dani was sun-worn and steady, caught between surfboards and custody schedules. He didn't offer forever—just a chair, a story, and half his heart.

Date 10
Ewan: The Scottish Riddle Man

There's a certain kind of man you meet at Bar Laval or in the Annex at dusk. The ones who speak in riddles, sip their mezcal like it's prophecy, and leave you wondering if you're flirting—or solving a puzzle.

Ewan was like that. All shine, all clever, all mirrors. From our first exchange, it felt like I was being interviewed for a role in his mythology. And I played along, of course. Who doesn't want to be the woman who finally cracks the enigma?

But this was the chapter I learned that shimmer isn't the same as substance. That a man can quote poetry, dress well, and make your brain dance—and still vanish when it's time to be real.

Not everything that glitters is gold. Sometimes, it's just the light playing tricks on your longing.

10 - Ewan:

Ewan was a handsome, Scottish-Canadian bartender in a fancy joint in Toronto. Medium build, fair skin, dark hair and eyes, and (swoon) a beard.

I had always been curious and intrigued about Scottish culture. In Brazil, we grow up hearing that Scots are great, knowledgeable farmers with a touch of mystical energy. Maybe it was just my imagination, but between crown ceremonies, ancient castles, and the Harry Potter magic, there's definitely something otherworldly about that culture. Maybe it's the Celtic background, the breathtaking landscapes, the storytelling... Whatever it was, I was hooked on his conversation like a fish on a hook, willing, wanting, and ready to be devoured.

Ewan noticed my curiosity, and it ignited something in him. He would take the most mundane things and turn them into epic tales. I loved it. It was like a brain exercise, but the fun kind. He also had a "nobody ever really listens to me" attitude, despite doing all the talking. It took me a little while to figure it out, but he wasn't being himself with me.

He was entertaining me, slipping into the server role he probably played every night. And being stuck in that role, even with someone he liked, clearly exhausted him. It was a little painful to watch.

Still, we chatted well enough. I had met him briefly at his workplace for an in-person introduction. It was quick, easy, and practical. We both agreed it was the best way. No major effort was needed if the attraction wasn't there. But the attraction was there—big time. So, we kept talking.

We weren't in a rush to meet again. Our conversations were deep, easy, and had a natural humor that made the hours fly. He was smart, witty, and refreshingly real. He was also an artist. He played guitar and was highly skilled with anything creative. I could easily imagine us at home, me cooking dinner while he strummed music in the background.

He had a simple but expectant heart, almost like a farmer spreading seeds with hope and faith in the harvest. It was beautiful and familiar to me. He was also the youngest of two brothers and had a complicated relationship with his parents, who had divorced when he was young.

His parents were highly academic with sharp minds and hard expectations. His choice to be a bartender, an artist, didn't exactly fit the family picture. That tension lingered in his life, and I could relate.

Finally, we managed to plan a real date. By then, it felt like our twentieth. We had already covered all the basics...and the advanced modules too. Conversation flowed effortlessly; laughter was natural. It was shaping up to be one of the smoothest, happiest starts I had had in a while.

And then—the bill came. Without skipping a beat, he abruptly asked the server to split it. I thought it was a little forceful, but hey, no big deal. Modern times, modern habits. But when the bill arrived, he pulled out a bag of coins. Quarters. Twenty-five-cent pieces. He started counting them, casually, deliberately.

I was... confused. And it wasn't about the money. He was a bartender. I knew tips came in coins. That wasn't the issue. It was how he did it. There was something odd, almost theatrical about it. He had a faint smirk, like a kid watching you try to solve a riddle he made up. I felt like I was being almost tested, in a Princess and the Pea kind of way. The meaning was there, behind it: I was being invited to pass a test I didn't even know I was supposed to take. Because I couldn't understand the necessity of the test at all, I was, apparently, already failing it. It felt surreal.

I could almost see the parallel reality unfolding—him as the husband, me as the wife, going through endless rounds of character testing and proving myself in ways I wouldn't even see coming. It wasn't about splitting the bill. It wasn't even about the coins. It was whatever deep, hidden criteria he had in his mind for choosing a partner. And I, unknowingly, was already flunking it.

Something turned off in me—fast and definitive. Maybe it was the fact that it wasn't about partnership but about endurance. Maybe it was the realization that whatever romance or laughter we shared would always carry an invisible scoreboard I never agreed to play by.

Whatever it was, it cooled my flame in a way that no other little misstep ever had. Needless to say, it was our first and last encounter.

Cultural Glimpse - The Scotsman

In Scotland, emotion hides behind weathered charm and dry wit. Men carry their hearts like old flasks—quiet, sturdy, never empty. Ewan didn't promise fireworks. He offered firewood. And in that stillness, I almost stayed.

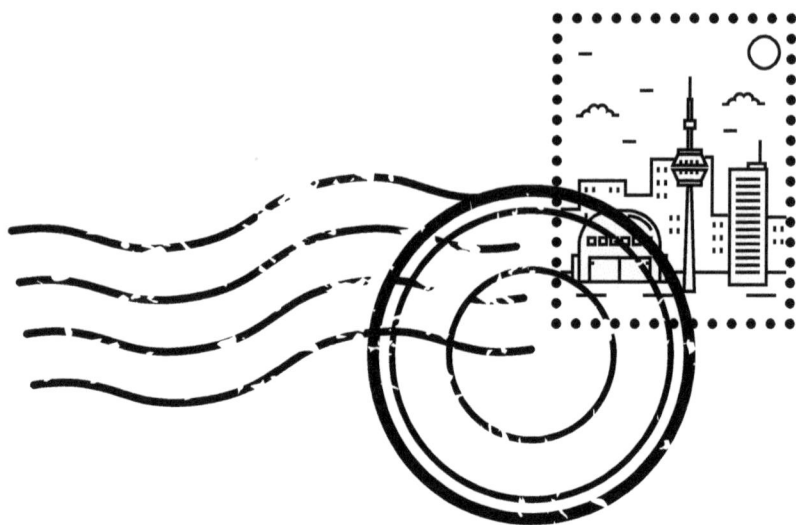

Date 11
Joe: The Sicilian Exorcism

Some men don't break your heart—they perform an exorcism on it.

Joe came wrapped in fantasy. Roses, champagne, grand gestures. A romance so cinematic it felt like it had been story-boarded by Fellini. But the thing about fantasies is this: if you don't know your own dream, someone else will sell you theirs.

This was the chapter where I almost bought the wrong dream. Where love was a performance, and I was cast in a role I didn't audition for. Where truth showed up in costume, and pain arrived dressed as devotion.

Joe reminded me: if you don't know what you're looking for, intensity can masquerade as intimacy. This wasn't heartbreak. This was awakening. And I left with something better than a love story—I left with myself.

11 - Joe:

Joe arrived at our date in a humongous truck. He was still perched up there when I spotted him, and right away, I caught the first lie: his height.

I should say, I wasn't particularly looking into anyone's height. Canadians are fairly tall, so when he said he was 175 cm, I didn't even think twice. In reality, he was a bit shorter, around my height. "In the smallest bottles, the strongest poisons," we say in Portuguese.

Our conversation started normally. And I can vouch that Italian is a love language. Italians know how to talk about love like no one else. Our banter was slow, steady, and almost shy. I wasn't in a hurry. Neither was he. We peeled layers like onions, little by little, which, if you know anything about Italians, was already a bit odd.

After my experience with Sean, who was very Catholic, I wondered if Joe had religious reservations. Maybe that's just how Italians wife-hunt. Who knows?

I was excited anyway. He was entertaining, and there was never a dull moment. Despite his first little lie, I hadn't spotted anything else suspicious. The chatting went on and on. I sensed he needed to know more and more about me. At one point, he even asked if I had childhood pictures. "As a movie producer, I'm fascinated by old photography," he explained. It made sense.

Joe built the sets for movies.

Before our first real date had even finished, we were already talking about family memories and baby photos. Interesting. I showed him a picture of me at a school graduation—face-up, pigtails, and red lipstick.

He was relieved. I didn't know what had shifted, but after that, it was like something unlocked inside him. He opened up. He became the real Italian lover I had imagined, maybe even better.

Joe also disclosed, on our first date, that he was a recovering alcoholic. I wasn't a heavy drinker myself, and having supported someone through recovery before, I jumped in with compassion and encouragement. He was thrilled.

Our first night together felt like a dream sequence from a movie. He pulled out his driver's license, right in front of me, took a photo of it, and said, "Send this to your girlfriends. I'm taking you to Niagara Falls for the weekend."

I was scared like a cat staring down a pack of dogs, but also incredibly excited. Trusting my instincts (and maybe the romantic glow of the moment), I agreed to join him. We drove to Niagara Falls.

The hotel was... holy moly. He built movie sets, after all. The room looked straight out of a Playboy Magazine fantasy: roses scattered everywhere, chocolates on the bed, champagne bottles chilling, dozens of candles burning. The smell of roses, candle wax, and champagne filled the air. It was intoxicating.

Part of me thought: This is a trap. Another part of me said: This is heaven. It ended up being one of the best nights of my life.

The next day, we woke up tangled together, not even bothering to leave the room.

He served me breakfast...with more champagne, of course. The royalty treatment didn't stop. Around lunchtime, he became more thoughtful. He started opening up even more, the way people sometimes do after too much happiness. Like he was searching for something to keep it real. He told me a story about the last time he had fallen in love, hard and fast, with an Asian woman. They had talked online for six months before she agreed to meet for a weekend getaway. He was completely besotted, even helping her financially during that time. He planned a perfect weekend for her, exactly the way he had for me: hotel, dinner, candles, champagne. He described it all in detail, proud of his orchestration and the love he had built. They stopped at a Shoppers Drug Mart on the way. She grabbed the biggest box of tampons she could find.

He chuckled, telling me he thought that, "A true warrior doesn't fear a bloody sword," as we say in Brazil. He even paid for it, laughing it off. They checked into the hotel. Had dinner. Candles. Music. Wine. Perfect. And then, as he kissed her and finally went to undress her—he discovered she had a penis.

He said something primal and terrifying rose up inside him. Animalistic rage. He managed to control himself—barely. He told her, "I'm leaving. Take your things and be gone when I come back, for both our sakes."

When he returned, she was gone, along with the box of tampons. Joe looked me straight in the eyes and said, almost whispering, "You saw how hard I go when I care."

No kidding. I had seen it. I sat there in silence. The weight of the story sat heavy between us. My heart broke a little: for him, for her, for me. We were all victims in some way of secrets, expectations, fear, and society's cruelty. I also thought about the unbelievable risk those women take, navigating a world that can be so dangerous for them. I pondered the cruelty of keeping something so essential hidden from someone investing deeply.

It was... a lot to carry and to process.

That night, Joe broke his sobriety. He disappeared for hours into the night. When he came back in the early morning, he was soaked in grandiose apologies and love-bombing. We had come in one car, so I agreed to return with him. He lived with his family in Oakville, something I only learned on the way back. I lived in Toronto. Halfway home, he asked if we could stop at his mother's house, just to lend her a hand with something. He added: "You'll love them."

Strangely, he looked... proud. Confused, exhausted, and still trying to make sense of everything, I agreed. It was a beautiful sunny afternoon. When we arrived, they welcomed me like family. His sister gave me a hug that felt like a secret message: You deserve better. I can't even explain it, but I felt it in my bones. I hugged her hard back.

His mother gave me some blessed bread—a holy wafer, she said, touched by the Pope himself. I took it, not out of belief, but as a symbolic gesture. It was a silent thank you to the universe for allowing me to walk away. It felt like a quiet benediction. The perfect Corpo de Cristo, fitting after what I could only describe as an exorcism of him, of me, of something we had no business calling love.

That was the last time I ever saw Joe.

Cultural Glimpse - The Sicilian

In Sicily, passion is inherited like land—fierce, sun-drenched, and full of ghosts. Love comes with loyalty, temper, and too much espresso. Joe moved like a man raised between saints and outlaws. Every touch was a vow. Every silence, a test.

Date 12
Armen: The Armenian Dream Husband

S
ome men arrive like a checklist in human form.
Armen was everything I was supposed to want: educated, kind, responsible, family-ready. A man who opened doors, made five-year plans, and never once forgot to ask how I slept. He was the kind of man who makes your aunties nod in approval and your therapist exhale in relief.

But sometimes, the perfect man on paper is just that—paper. And when you place it beside your soul, it doesn't light up. This was the chapter I learned the difference between being wanted and being understood. Between having a future with someone and actually feeling it. Armen was lovely. He really was. But you can't build a life on lovely alone.

Toronto taught me this in quiet corners: on café patios in Yorkville, on silent walks past Trinity Bellwoods, watching couples who looked perfect—but never touched. This was the chapter I realized: Being someone's dream doesn't mean you're living yours.

12 - Armen:

I grew up in São Paulo, a city that thrives on diversity. It's a place where cultures collide and intertwine seamlessly, like different threads woven together into a vibrant tapestry. Mixing cultures isn't simply normal there, it's encouraged. People don't bat an eye when you bring someone from a different background into your life. In fact, it's practically expected. São Paulo does more than embrace diversity—it celebrates it, with arms wide open.

Take the Armenians, for example. After the Armenian Genocide in the early 20th century, many Armenians fled their homeland, seeking refuge in Brazil. São Paulo became home to a significant number of them, and their community grew quietly but steadily. Their resilience in the face of tragedy, their rich culture, and their traditions became a vital part of the city's makeup. Yet, in São Paulo, this wasn't something you'd ever really notice unless you were paying attention. The Armenian community fit in naturally among the city's eclectic mix, like just another flavor in the melting pot.

I didn't know much about the specifics of their history growing up, but I knew that Armenians were proud of their roots. They had a reputation for being close-knit and holding onto their cultural traditions with tenacity. Yes, there were whispers about how they valued keeping things within their community and how their families were sometimes less than thrilled with outsiders. But São Paulo doesn't care much about keeping things within the lines. Mixing cultures was and still is the heartbeat of the city. For me, that was just the way things were.

Fast forward to Toronto, where my life had taken an unexpected turn after Joe. If Joe was a whirlwind of mistakes and lessons learned, then Armin was the perfect calm after the storm. Armin was magnetic, the kind of person you couldn't help but notice when he walked into the room. He was charming... and irresistible.

Armen was a shoe salesman. I know it sounds a little... unremarkable, but he made it seem like the most important job in the world. In his hands, it really was. He had this way of fitting shoes that made you feel like you weren't just buying footwear but investing in a whole new identity. His customers would leave the store floating a little higher, their backs straighter, their confidence boosted. Armen was the kind of guy who didn't just sell shoes; he made you want them, even if you had no intention of buying anything when you walked in.

I used to call him my "Cinderella maker." And trust me, he was. He had the whole package—smooth as butter, always impeccably dressed in a way that made him look like he belonged in a fashion magazine. This guy didn't just wear clothes; he wore them. He had an effortless style, a mix of tailored suits and casual finesse, like he'd walked straight out of an Arabian Nights tale and ended up strolling the streets of Toronto. And let's not forget the scent. He always smelled amazing—like the cologne section in a department store, but in the best way possible. It wasn't overbearing, just... perfect.

Oh, and the generosity. Armen was the kind of guy who couldn't show up empty-handed. If we went to dinner, he'd bring a gift. A bouquet of flowers, a little trinket from some exotic store, something that said, "I was thinking of you." I'm not talking about extravagant, over--the-top presents. There were thoughtful, little things that made you feel like you were important and mattered. Armen's charm wasn't in what he gave; it was in how he made you feel like you were the most important person in the room, whether he'd known you for five minutes or five years.

My friends adored him. Armen was like a politician in a constant campaign—always working the room, knowing exactly what to say, when to laugh, and when to lean in just a little closer to make you feel like you were his best friend. He had this way of making everything feel like an adventure, like you were part of some amazing, thrilling story where the plot twisted at every turn.

But even though we got along like peas in a pod, there was an undeniable weight to the relationship. Armen and I both knew it. I met his family eventually, and while they were kind and welcoming, you could feel the gravity of their cultural expectations. Family was everything to them. You don't just marry anyone when you're Armenian. You marry within the community. There were unspoken rules about how to behave. I could see that Armen, despite his easy charm and laid-back style, was carrying the weight of those expectations. I don't think either of us was prepared to bear it.

It wasn't that his family didn't like me—it wasn't about that. It was the unspoken rules that we both couldn't quite fit into. It was the pressure of trying to meet the expectations that we both knew deep down weren't our own, but those of a culture that had endured so much and held on to its traditions with pride.

While I respected and admired that, deep down, I knew that no matter how strong our connection was, we couldn't sustain the weight of those cultural expectations without losing ourselves in the process.

We didn't fight. We didn't argue. We just knew. The unspoken truth was there, like a silent understanding between us. This was a great story, but it wasn't going to last forever. Our love, while real, was just a chapter in our lives, one that would end when we each had to go our separate ways to build the life that was meant for us.

I wouldn't have changed a thing. I'll always look back on my time with Armin as one of those great experiences you don't get very often. He was a whirlwind of charm and laughter, a rare and unforgettable adventure. He taught me that sometimes, a relationship doesn't need to last forever to be valuable. Sometimes, it's just about enjoying the ride while it lasts, and when it ends, knowing that you've both learned something from the journey.

Armen and I didn't last. But that didn't mean we didn't matter. He was a part of my life when I needed someone like him, and I was a part of his. We weren't meant to be forever, but we were meant to be, for a time. And that, in the end, was enough.

Cultural Glimpse – The Armenian

In Armenia, love is inherited through resilience, faith, and old grief. Men grow up with history in their bones and duty on their shoulders. Armen's hands were gentle, and he didn't say much, but his gaze carried centuries.

Date 13
Ali: The Afghan-German Drift

Ali was like a man driving from Toronto to Hamilton without ever deciding which exit to take. Gentle, poetic, intriguing—just not going anywhere. The kind of guy who thinks emotional proximity counts as commitment, as if being sensitive means he's not still wasting your time.

13 - Ali:

Some matches you swipe on with your fingers. Others, you feel in your spine.

Ali was one of those uncanny repetitions of the universe—physically, he looked almost exactly like Armen. The same charming eyes, the same angular jawline, even the same warm, slightly mysterious energy. I was stunned when I saw his picture. Was this a glitch in the matrix? Or just Toronto being Toronto again, playing roulette with the world's DNA?

Ali was Afghan-German. That alone made him intriguing. My curiosity was piqued—not because of his resemblance to Armen (okay, maybe a little), but because I sensed he was carrying a duality within him. A man of East and West. Tea and techno. Poetic heritage and practical precision.

Our conversations started slow, like a match struggling to catch flame. He was thoughtful, careful, and not the type to overshare, which I respected. But as we talked more, I discovered that behind his slightly guarded posture, there was a man full of internal dialogue. Ali was carrying layers of culture, displacement, and effort. And I love a good peeling session.

Unlike Armen, Ali didn't try to charm me with big gestures or loud confidence. He had the softness of someone raised on expectations and history. He was the kind of man who doesn't just answer a question but contemplates its moral weight first. I was fascinated.

He told me about growing up in Germany, in a tight Afghan diaspora community where honor was currency and tradition wasn't optional. But Ali was a modern man, or at least trying to be. He had built a life for himself in Toronto that had nothing to do with war or exile or cultural debt. And yet, those things lived in him and shaped him.

Sometimes, I'd catch a glint of sadness in his tone when we talked about home. Which one? That was always the question. Kabul? Hamburg? Mississauga?

One night, over shisha and black tea on a patio downtown, he asked me what it was like to be a woman raised between two worlds, Brazil and Canada. I laughed. "Loud and confusing," I said. But I knew what he meant. We were both living stories that didn't have ready-made endings.

Ali didn't try to impress me. He invited me into silence. Into pauses. Into realness. And yet, there was something... unfinished between us.

He confessed, weeks into our friendship-turned-almost-romance, that he was still holding out hope to one day marry someone from his culture who his family could embrace. "Someone who understands," he said, with a quiet apology built into his voice.

I did understand. That the world he came from still had a grip on his freedom. That identity and loyalty are sometimes heavier than attraction and curiosity.

Ali was a mirror—one that reflected both my open-mindedness and my limits. He taught me that not all connections are meant to bloom into love. Some just reveal truths. His came gently, like a wave that touches your feet but never takes you in.

I never kissed Ali. But I held his story close, like a quiet revolution.

Cultural Glimpse - The Afghan-German

In Kabul, loyalty is survival. In Berlin, independence is law. Ali carried both: discipline in his spine, poetry in his pause. He was not torn. He was braided. A man who loved in theory, but never in surrender.

Date 14
Savvas: The Greek Sphinx

Toronto teaches you early on: culture is not costume. It's coded into food, silence, family dynamics, and flirtation. Especially flirtation.

Savvas knew this. Greek, magnetic, and impossibly smooth, he wore his cultural pride like cologne—thick, noticeable, intoxicating. At first, it smelled like depth. Like passion marinated in centuries of Mediterranean mythology. And I, ever the curious one, wanted to know all the ingredients. He complimented my culture. Asked questions. Spoke with reverence about femininity, motherhood, migration. He seemed aware. And if there's one thing that makes a modern woman lower her guard, it's a man who appears culturally sensitive.

But here's the thing they don't always tell you: cultural sensitivity can be a seduction strategy. And charm, when used expertly, can double as camouflage. This was the chapter I realized: not every man who reveres your roots will protect your boundaries.

Savvas taught me that knowing how to speak your language—literally or emotionally—is not the same as honoring it. That a man can say all the right things in five different languages, and still mean none of them when the lights go down.

In Toronto, where cultures brush shoulders in coffee shops and bed sheets, it's easy to confuse curiosity for respect. I learned the difference the hard way. This wasn't just a love story. It was a wake-up call—with an accent.

14 - Savvas:

Savvas was as mysterious as he was sexy. He was tall, with a short, army-style haircut, and a clean shave that would make Michelangelo's angels jealous. Dark-skinned, medium build, all wrapped up in the perfect upgraded model of a good, fun, and unpredictable husband. He had a kind of kinetic beauty. You could feel it moving around him like a magnetic field.

Savvas was something else entirely. This guy was so incredibly mysterious that on our first date, before the appetizers even landed, he gave me a fifteen-minute speech about how he had once left a date through the back door of a restaurant. She had done something that, according to him, deserved the Houdini act. He said it like he was proud of it, like he was giving me a warning and a promise at the same time.

And then, to make it even weirder, he left his keys and wallet on the table as proof that he trusted me.

No one had asked for proof. Not me, not the waiter, not the universe. But there they were. His sacred worldly possessions, staring at me like confused little witnesses.

Savvas was like that, offering proof I never requested, dropping receipts for loyalty before I could even ask his middle name. "I'm messaging you on a Friday night," he'd say with a little smirk. "See? I'm into you. Not out there with other women." Or, "I'm here with you, not at a bar. Look."

It was... confusing, like trying to learn philosophy drunk. And then, poof, he would disappear—gone like a magician's rabbit, leaving behind only a faint smell of expensive cologne and more questions than answers. Then he would pop back into my life again, like nothing happened. His disappearances always came with some kind of Savvas-style explanation—something that, at least to him, made perfect sense. He would talk about "needing to clear the mind" or "the moon cycles" or "bad energies," and, honestly, part of me didn't mind it.

It was like I had been invited to one of those murder mystery dinner parties where you're supposed to pick up clues and solve the story before dessert. I was the detective, and Savvas was every suspicious character rolled into one, serving me riddles with a side of Greek charm.

At the back of my mind, though, I started seeing patterns. Growing up in Brazil, where violence is a different kind of everyday presence, you learn to spot signs and behaviors. My friends who are police officers taught me to always trust the small, weird things. The unnecessary tests. The sudden withdrawals. The elaborate speeches that no one asked for.

It didn't feel dangerous, but it felt... calculated. I wasn't scared, but I was paying attention. Then came the moment that sealed Savvas in my memory forever. We were having a casual coffee date when he leaned forward across the table with the kind of serious face you see in spy movies, and asked, "Is your mother fat?"

I didn't know how to respond. "What?"

"Is your mother fat?" he repeated, slower this time, like maybe I didn't hear the absurdity the first time.

I thought he was joking. I full-belly laughed, head tilted back and hand on my heart. I thought it was a setup for a punchline.

He didn't laugh. Instead, he gave me the solemn, almost pitying look you give someone who doesn't understand something sacred. Savvas went on to explain, dead serious, that it was a Greek belief that a woman would "become" her mother's body type. If a woman's mother was overweight, it was not just probable, it was fated that the daughter would end up the same.

"It's important," he said gravely. "My mother wouldn't forgive me if I brought home someone who was going to get fat."

The silence after that was so thick you could slice it with a knife.

I don't remember exactly what I said, but internally, something clicked. There it was: the moment you feel the romance air leak out of the room like a slow, invisible deflation. You don't even panic. You just watch it happen, knowing it can't be undone.

I realized, in that instant, that Savvas wasn't trying to date a woman. He was trying to solve an equation. Trying to predict the future with insurance policies and ancient body myths. And worse—he thought this was normal.

For the rest of the coffee, I watched him—the perfect face, the magnetic pull, the weird loyalty proofs, the sudden absences all rearranging themselves in my mind as a flashing neon sign that said: Not for you.

Still, I stayed polite. I finished my drink and smiled, but I knew I wouldn't see him again.

Savvas was a beautiful chapter. A mystery novel that started with magic and ended with a heavy thud of real life. A reminder that even the most dazzling exteriors can hide deal-breakers under a polished surface. And maybe some mysteries aren't meant to be solved.

Cultural Glimpse - The Greek

In Greece, love is a storm sung in myth—loud, magnetic, unforgettable. Men flirt like philosophers and vanish like legends. Savvas didn't walk. He arrived with heat, hunger, and prophecy. But even the gods grow quiet when the charm fades.

Date 15
Sri: @Virgen29 – The Uniform of Grace

Some men arrive like prayers, not to be answered, but to remind us we're heard. Sri never promised anything. He didn't chase or charm. He just appeared—like light through blinds, steady and unannounced. He walked the city with a heart so quiet it echoed.

He carried his duty like poetry. Not loud. Not performative. Just... present. Toronto's sirens softened near him. Its corners felt less sharp. He wasn't my lover. He was my pause. A moment of peace between storms. The kind of man who doesn't ask for trust, but earns it without trying.

I never dreamed of a life with him. But I never doubted he was part of mine. He taught me that love doesn't always come with fireworks. Sometimes, it wears a uniform. Sometimes, it just holds the line—gently, faithfully, and without applause. And that, too, is worth writing down.

15 - Sri:

Sri was one of those guys the algorithm simply forgot. With a nickname like @Virgen29, maybe the algorithm was doing him a favor. I had seen his profile a few times during my early days of online dating, just floating there like a lonely balloon in the internet sky.

Like most women, I had mixed feelings about it. But the social scientist in me got curious. Instead of ignoring him, I decided to fish out an old, unanswered message he had sent me months before: Hey, how are you?

It was simple and innocent, from a time before AI-generated novellas clogged the apps with fake chemistry. A little fossil of a real human attempt. So, I replied.

He responded quickly and thoughtfully, referencing something specific from my profile. He was a real person. Imagine that.

Unable to resist teasing him a little, I asked: "Are you looking for someone to deflower you?"

He didn't seem to be offended at all. "Not necessarily," he replied. "I'm Sri Lankan, and I hope to share that moment with my future wife, yes."

Wait. Wasn't virginity supposed to be something women hid either because they had it, or because they didn't? What was a grown man doing announcing it proudly, wearing it like a badge? At first, I didn't know what to make of him.

But curiosity kicked in again, along with respect. That conversation, which started half as a joke, grew into a real friendship.

Sri was deeply spiritual, but not the Instagram kind of "spiritual" we see everywhere now. Sri was Sikh. His faith taught him that service to others wasn't a way of life. Seva, they call it. Selfless service. Protection of the weak. Truthfulness, courage, humility. Everything we dream of finding in the people who are supposed to look after society, but so rarely do.

Over time, he told me more about himself. He'd been online dating since he was 29, and now, at 35, he had pretty much given up on the whole idea of finding love online.

His profile didn't even attract scammers. "Not even the bots wanted me!" he said once, laughing hard.

It was heartbreaking and funny at the same time, the way a lot of honest things are. Somewhere along the way, Sri became my trusted advisor, my unofficial Dating Yoda. Whenever I matched with someone new, I would send Sri a screenshot of the guy's profile. Not to gossip or mock, but to get a second opinion from someone who had no skin in the game.

Sri could spot red flags I missed. He would point out the small tells: the overly curated selfies, the profiles where men described their perfect woman but said nothing about themselves, the "casual" photos that screamed of commitment issues.

He taught me what to look for, not just in photos, but in tone and patterns. "Watch how fast they escalate the conversation," he'd say. "Good men don't need to rush. They build."

When AI exploded and online dating became even more of a minefield, I realized how precious those lessons were.

But back then, before AI, it was still possible to believe you were talking to a real, imperfect, breathing human being. It was messy, confusing, and wonderful. And Sri was there, patiently guiding me through it.

Through all this, I learned that Sri was a Toronto Police Officer. It made perfect sense. Sikhism teaches that protecting others is sacred and that courage without ego is the ideal. For Sikhs, justice isn't something you study; it's something you live, every day, even when no one is watching.

In my mind, he became like one of those small-town sheriffs you see in old Westerns—steady, respectful, and unfussy. The guy who would show up if you needed help and actually listen.

He didn't date much. He didn't seem to mind. He spent his weekends with his parents, his neighbors, and the community. He belonged to the quiet corners of the city that most people didn't notice, and kept them safe without needing applause for it.

I used to tease him that if he ever wanted to finally lose his virginity, he should go to Brazil. "If you're gonna learn, you might as well learn from the experts," I said.

We laughed a lot—always with love and mutual respect. We never dated. We never even flirted seriously. Our bond was different. He was like a lighthouse, standing firm when my emotions, my fears, and my hopes were tossing me around.

When my birthday rolled around, he came to my party. He was quiet, polite, and friendly. He blended in like he'd always been there.

Later that night, he met the man who would eventually become my husband. He shook his hand, smiled, and gave me a small, secret thumbs-up from across the room. It meant more to me than I could say.

Today, when I read the news about the growing violence in Toronto, when I hear people talk about the police with such anger and sadness, I think about Sri. I think about the men and women like him who you don't notice because they're not loud, flashy, or looking for trouble. They're just there, standing guard at the edge of the chaos to protect others with compassion and without fear. And Sri, with his quiet faith and even quieter strength, was one of the finest examples I ever met.

Cultural Glimpse - The Sri Lankan

In Sri Lanka, emotion simmers beneath tradition, carried in food, ritual, and restraint. Sri split atoms by day and wrote poems by night— logic and longing, side by side. He didn't fall in love. He observed it. Like code, like art, like a language he almost trusted.

Date 16
Steve: The Man from the North

I f someone had told me that, in the midst of my love study, I would find answers among pine trails and vintage car hoods in Barrie, I would've laughed.

Not out of arrogance — but out of ignorance. The kind of ignorance polished by big city life, by theory, by lovers who speak too loudly and touch too little. That soft, progressive ignorance that mistakes quiet for lack and simplicity for delay. Steve didn't come to teach me anything. And maybe that's why I learned so much. He didn't talk about masculinity. He embodied it — unknowingly. Without applause. Without apology.

In his quiet presence, I realized how much the world had trained me to listen for performances — and how far I'd drifted from hearing what makes no sound.

Steve was a trail off the map. A detour that, without trying, led me back to something essential: The idea that not all love has to be complex to be true. There were no grand promises, no curated quotes. Just mustard on fingers, soulful engines, and a rare kind of attention that doesn't rush. And maybe — just maybe — love is also this: A man who doesn't try to decipher you. And still, somehow, sees you.

16 - Steve

If you had told me I'd drive up to Barrie to meet a "redneck," I might have packed a guidebook and a compass like I was off to spot an Amazonian mermaid.

Growing up in South America, the idea of a "redneck" was as mythical to me as pink dolphins or jungle witches. It was something you heard about, maybe laughed about, but never someone you expected to have coffee with.

Then came Steve.

When he pulled up in his red truck to our hiking date, it was almost cinematic. His look was complete with a red flannel shirt, a black Pantera T-shirt underneath, beat-up Converse sneakers, and a quiet half-smile. He looked exactly like his three online photos.

Steve was, refreshingly, exactly who he said he was. He was tall and lean, built like a man who had split wood most of his life and never set foot inside a yoga studio. His business was simple: he cleaned windows. Summers were busy; winters were for staying home. No networking events, no side hustles selling motivational seminars. Just life, stripped down to the essentials. In a world that sometimes feels like it's trying too hard, Steve's simplicity was intriguing.

When we met, I couldn't stop talking (typical). I asked him about everything, including his music, his truck, and his hometown. I also probed why his online profile only had three pictures, and why none of them showed him smiling properly.

Steve mostly answered with shrugs, soft chuckles, and one-liners that carried more weight than whole essays.

"You're quiet," I finally said, halfway up a hiking trail.

He grinned and said, "You're not."

Touché.

We climbed higher into the woods, and I realized how much he loved the outdoors. The way he pointed out things—a hawk circling overhead, the rustle of a rabbit through the underbrush—it wasn't performative. He wasn't trying to impress me. This was just his language. Slowly, quietly, I started to understand: Steve wasn't a man of words but a man of sensing.

Later, we headed into town for the vintage car show. That's where I saw Steve come alive. He moved among the old Chevys, Fords, and Dodges with a reverence usually reserved for cathedrals. He told me which years were the best for carburetors. He explained why certain curves in old metal bodies were "just sexy." (His words.) He waxed almost poetic about why a '67 Mustang would always be superior to any new muscle car "because soul don't come out of a factory, sweetheart."

I laughed, genuinely. I learned more about carburetors that afternoon than I knew about my own country's political scandals.

It was a language I didn't speak, but one I could appreciate, because he spoke it with such love.

We ended the day at a local hot dog stand, the kind of place that's been there since before Instagram existed and doesn't care if you hashtag it. Steve ordered "the usual" and didn't bother explaining it. He just handed me a loaded hot dog, dripping mustard onto my fingers, and said: "Best thing you'll eat all day. Trust."

He was right. As we sat on the curb, eating messy hot dogs and wiping mustard off our jeans, I looked over and asked, half-teasing, "So... are you really a redneck?"

Steve leaned back on his elbows, squinting into the late afternoon sun. He shrugged, gave that easy, almost boyish grin, and said, "If that's what you wanna call it."

There was no shame or irony in his tone. It was like he was handing me the word, saying, "Here. You figure it out." Gradually, I did figure it out. Steve wasn't a caricature or a punchline.

He was simple, proud, and a little rough around the edges, but deeply kind. He was history. He had layers of post-war struggles, small-town pride, handed-down music tastes and traditions, all carried quietly, without needing to be explained or defended.

He didn't fit labels or run from them either. He just lived quietly, authentically.

Meeting Steve broke something in me: the reflex to label what I didn't understand. It made me realize that the people we mock or fear from a distance are usually just people carrying their own histories and quiet dignities, the best way they can.

Steve wasn't trying to impress the world. He wasn't selling anything. He was simply being, and in today's world, that's almost revolutionary.

Somewhere between the trail and the carburetors and the hot dog mustard, Steve taught me something I didn't even know I needed: That real strength doesn't always wear a power suit. Sometimes it wears flannel and old Converse and drives a beat-up truck, and still shows up, fully, genuinely, without a script.

Steve left me with many lessons, but the one I carry most is this: If you look for the right thing, you'll find it. Everyone has a light, ready to ignite—if you let go of the labels long enough to see it.

Cultural Glimpse: The Quiet North

He wasn't exotic. He was the kind of man I was taught to overlook: White, small-town, and flannel-wearing. But Steve wasn't a stereotype. He was a reminder that not all stories come with subtitles. Some men love better in silence than others do in poetry.

Date 17
Mike: The Roman Gravedigger of Chaos

Toronto has many ghosts—old lovers, forgotten texts, subway flings lost between Spadina and Union. But Mike? Mike didn't haunt me. He buried the ghosts. He was the gravedigger of chaos. Not the dark, spooky kind. The municipal worker kind. The one who shows up at 7 a.m. with a thermos of calm and says, "Let's clean this mess up."

Mike was kindness with a shovel. A man who arrived when I was still dancing with the drama, still addicted to the spark of men who didn't know how to spell "emotional availability," let alone practice it. He didn't chase. He stayed. He didn't ignite me—he grounded me. And in a city that teaches women to want the flame, that's confusing.

It took me years to realize that love doesn't have to be a wildfire. Sometimes it's a well-dug garden bed. Mike asked questions. Real ones. He took out his heart like a mechanic pulls open a hood gently, precisely, offering it for inspection. I wasn't ready. But I remember it.

Because somewhere in between his steady laughter and Saturday brunch plans, I saw it: The map. Not of a perfect man. But of what peace might look like, if I ever got brave enough to stop running. He didn't write poems. He built compost bins and he taught me that sometimes, the sexiest thing a man can offer... is stability.

And that, darling, is how Mike helped me start burying my old taste in men.

17 - Mike:

Sri had been a balm for my soul after Joe. His kindness, his loyalty, and his very existence had been invaluable in helping me heal. Having a real, honest-to-God friend who happened to be a Toronto Police Officer, Sikh, and the human version of chamomile tea was exactly what I needed.

But now that I was happy again—healed, whole, and a little wiser—I was ready to choose badly on purpose. I wanted something casual. Or, as we Brazilians say, a "pau amigo," a friend with benefits. No strings. No dreams. No "where is this going?" talks. Just laughs, kisses, maybe some motorcycle rides, and a little chaos. Pure vacation for the heart.

That's when I met Mike. Mike was a Roman from Rome. Not "my--grandparents-were-Italian" Roman. Mike spoke with the kind of rugged Roman accent that sounded like it was carved into stone centuries ago. He was anti-Catholic and anti-tourist.

Mike had the build of a Roman soldier you'd see in a museum: Broad shoulders, dirt-blonde hair, fair Mediterranean skin, and a voice so deep and rough it could sand wood. Of course, he had a motorcycle. The Universe clearly wanted me to make bad decisions in style.

When he messaged me, I replied without hesitation. I was in the mood for some trouble, and Mike looked like trouble on two wheels.

Before I go further, you need to know: Brazil is home to the second-largest Italian community outside of Italy. Where I grew up, in São Paulo, Italian was almost a second language. We had Italian schools, Italian bakeries, and entire neighborhoods that smelled like fresh gnocchi. I even knew how to sing an entire song in Italian—although, to be fair, it was mostly because of the Italian soap operas we all watched. Culturally speaking, Italians and Brazilians are cousins who party together at every family gathering.

So, when Mike and I started talking, it felt easy, familiar, and effortless. The conversation flowed. He told me about growing up in Rome and how much he hated what tourism had done to his city. How the crowds and the commercialization had pushed real Romans to the margins, turning sacred spaces into Instagram backdrops.

I loved hearing him rant—the raw honesty and bitterness wrapped in a Roman shrug.

It made him real.

Then he dropped the bomb: "I'm a gravedigger."

For a solid minute, I thought he was joking. When I realized he wasn't, my brain short-circuited in a very practical, weird way. I wasn't creeped out, I has a firefighter after all, but I had lots of questions, though:

Wait, is it cold? What do they do in winter?

How deep are the graves?

Do you need a special license for that?

The more he talked, the more I realized something unexpected: Mike wasn't my guy. Don't get me wrong, he was ridiculously hot. But as I listened to him talk about death metal concerts, underground art scenes, and his disdain for organized anything, a different thought popped into my mind: Oh my God. I know his soulmate. Her name was Kizita. She loved gore, heavy metal, dark humor, and horror movies.

Kizita once told me that her ideal man would be someone who could quote Edgar Allan Poe while riding a motorcycle into a thunderstorm.

Mike was basically her Pinterest board made flesh. Without even thinking, I blurted it out: "You need to meet my friend."

Mike froze. He looked confused and maybe a little offended. I could almost see the gears grinding in his head: Was this a rejection? Was I calling him ugly?

I quickly explained. "Listen, she's not looking for you either. This isn't about desperation. I just think you two might... explode beautifully."

He raised an eyebrow. I raised both hands in mock surrender. "Let me check with her first. But I'm telling you: if you two meet, you're doomed in the best possible way."

Reluctantly, Mike agreed. I messaged Kizita, who, knowing me, wasn't surprised at all.

"Send me his picture," she said, laughing.

When she saw it—180 centimeters of pure muscle, bad boy energy, and a motorcycle that looked like it had survived the apocalypse, she burst out laughing.

Then I dropped the final bomb. "Oh, by the way, he's a gravedigger."

"Are you trying to marry me off to the Grim Reaper?"

I laughed. But underneath it, I knew: this was it. Sometimes, you just feel it. The right person at the right time.

I went back to Mike and arranged the meeting. And I'm happy to report: They dated for a while. Turns out, the universe doesn't just send you what you want. Sometimes, it sends you what someone else needs and uses you as the courier.

That night, sipping my wine, feeling all smug about my matchmaking skills, I thought: Maybe bad choices aren't always bad. Sometimes they're just redirected blessings.

Cultural Glimpse - The Roman

In Rome, charm is an inheritance, and seduction a civic duty. Love is loud, layered, and often late but always dressed well. Mike had the swagger of a Vespa and the heart of a son who called his mother daily. He kissed like it was Sunday mass with ritual, reverence, and mischief.

Date 18
Daniel: The Portuguese Historian

Some men know history. Fewer are ready to stand up and change it.

Daniel was a man of memory—an archivist of feeling. He knew the lineage of every battle, every loss. Portuguese blood, old soul, soft voice. The kind of man who could quote revolutions but hesitated at the thought of one in his own life.

We'd meet near the University of Toronto, his hands always holding a book, mine holding questions. He told stories like scripture, with reverence. But when it came to our story, he stayed quiet. As if rewriting the script was betrayal.

This was the chapter where I realized that knowing the past is not the same as healing it. And that sometimes, good men get stuck between what was—and what could be. Daniel taught me the language of reflection. But I needed the courage of change. And Toronto? It stayed honest. Unapologetic. A city that lets you choose—root deeper or grow elsewhere.

18 - Daniel:

It all started with a message and an opening line so elegant and grammatically impeccable it could've been written by the ghost of Camões himself. That alone caught my attention. Not because I expected poor grammar, but because perfect Portuguese, particularly from a man, is often a flex of education, culture, and maybe even a little bit of pride. Daniel had all three.

He was a historian—reserved, soft-spoken, and carried himself with that "Clark Kent before he flies" kind of aura. He had a medium build, black-framed glasses, and a gaze that didn't seek approval, just understanding. That was the first clue: this man wasn't your typical Portuguese guy. He didn't have the bravado, the heavy flirtation, or that soccer-charged patriotism. No. Daniel was intellectual, polite, and quietly intense.

I have Portuguese roots myself. My grandfather was Portuguese, and although he was the kindest grandpa, legend has it he wasn't the best husband. My grandmother died in childbirth at 40, and her story remained a wound in the family tree, passed down in whispers and weighted glances. So, when Daniel appeared, part of me was skeptical. The other part was starved for brain sex.

And brain sex we had.

We debated everything—colonialism, revolutions, battle strategies, sugar cane trade routes. He brought the historical records, and I brought post-colonial lived experience. I was the descendant of a land that had been invaded and "civilized." He, the keeper of its archives.

I challenged him, often and loudly. He never flinched. Instead, he listened, countered, and at times, conceded. That felt like intimacy to me. Not just being heard, but intellectually wrestled with. It was thrilling. Our chemistry existed entirely in dialogue, sometimes flirtatious, mostly electric in the space between facts and feelings.

Daniel had type 1 diabetes, something I found out only when he nearly collapsed during one of our long walks. I'd noticed the sweating, the slurring—signs I knew too well from my firefighter training. I had to force sugar into his mouth while he protested weakly that he was fine. After he stabilized, he admitted he had tried to hide it.

"I didn't want you to see me as fragile," he said, eyes downcast.

But I didn't see fragility. I saw denial. And I didn't love that.

Still, we pressed on. Eventually, I met his friends, a lively bunch of expats and new immigrants, most of them Portuguese. They were warm, curious, loud, and deeply nostalgic for a homeland that had grown shinier the farther it drifted into memory.

That's when it happened. We were gathered in a backyard in Toronto, a few bottles of vinho verde into the evening, when one of Daniel's friends, an older man with slicked-back grey hair and a baritone laugh, handed me a small package. Inside, there was a wooden pendant. A deep, dark red.

"Here," he said with a grin. "Pau-Brasil. A little souvenir from the motherland. So you Brazilians can stop complaining and finally take it back."

Laughter erupted. I froze. Let me explain. Pau-Brasil is more than just wood. It's history. It's blood. It's the reason Brazil was named Brazil. The tree, harvested obsessively by Portuguese colonizers in the 16th century, was nearly driven to extinction. Its red dye, used in Europe's elite textiles, became a symbol of the wealth sucked out of Brazilian soil—just one of many treasures extracted with no intention of return. The forest, the people, the languages, the souls. Colonization wasn't just a moment. It's a scar.

Now, here I was, being handed a polished slice of it like a cute joke. Something in me snapped. I stared at the man and, without raising my voice, said:

"Giving back something that was stolen isn't a gift. It's called restitution. And by the way, I am Portuguese, too. You taught me that, remember?"

Silence. Thick as molasses. I didn't wait for a reaction. I grabbed the pendant, slipped it into my bag, and walked out of the backyard. My face was calm. My body was trembling.

Daniel ran after me. "Wait," he said, "he was joking."

"I know," I said. "That's what made it worse."

And I meant it. Jokes are supposed to be harmless. But colonization isn't harmless. It's generational, relational, cellular. It lives in language, in property lines, in last names. It lives in me. I was raised in a country where the indigenous population was decimated, where Afro-Brazilian religions were demonized, where we joke about colonizers because the truth still burns.

Daniel didn't say anything right away. His silence wasn't defensive, but it was heavy with thought.

Later, he apologized. Not for his friend—because you can't apologize for someone else—but for not anticipating the weight of that moment. For not seeing that, for me, Pau-Brasil wasn't a symbol of cultural unity. It was a reminder of loss.

We didn't date much longer after that because the illusion of shared identity had cracked. I realized I was still looking for someone who didn't need a history lesson to understand where I stood. Daniel was brilliant, kind, and possibly still thinks of me when he sees a necklace.

Cultural Glimpse - The Portuguese

In Portugal, longing is a language spoken in Fado, in wine, and in unfinished goodbyes. History isn't past there, it's personal. Daniel loved like a scholar: carefully, passionately, and with a reverence for ruin. Even his silence had footnotes.

Date 19
David: The Dominican Chef

S ome men feed your stomach. David fed my nervous system.
There's a kind of love that doesn't make big speeches. It stirs the beans. It picks up the kids. It remembers how you take your coffee, and then brings it. That's David. I met him during a season of romantic indigestion. I had too many fast flings and too many microwaved affections and then David walked in with his calm voice, slow hands, and rice that never stuck to the bottom of the pot.

A Dominican single dad raising three daughters? Sister, I should've left right then before I fell in love with the whole family. He didn't wine and dine me—he seasoned and simmered. His way of flirting? Feeding me second helpings and asking how my week was. His sex appeal? Doing bedtime routines like a bedtime god. Honestly, it was rude how good he made "regular" look. But there was a moment—probably somewhere between the stewed chicken and his oldest daughter's math homework—when I realized: I wasn't ready to be someone's fourth priority. Not because I needed to be first. But because I wanted to be chosen, not inherited.

David wasn't my person. But he reminded me what peace smelled like—like garlic and cumin and good intentions. And for that, he'll always have a warm pot on the stove in my heart.

19 - David:

David sent me a respectful message. There were no games, no half--jokes, and no "hey sexy" energy. He was a real man, upfront and a dad of three little girls who, by some strange magic, even looked a little like me.

Most women in my position would've run away. Three kids? Divorced? Busy schedule? Massive emotional baggage? I didn't run. I ran toward it. Maybe it was my cultural roots. Maybe it was my spiritual upbringing. Maybe it was societal expectations, or maybe, my own stubborn heart. Something about David gave me a feeling of giving back to the universe.

I grew up watching my father raise three kids on his own after my mother left. Later, my stepmother, a courageous woman, joined him and took on the task with open arms. She made it work.

I guess deep down, I believed that if you wanted something badly enough, if you believed in it hard enough, you could build a family with your own hands.

David was from the Dominican Republic. Short, lean, and athletic, he had a runner's build. In his youth, he had been a baseball player, and he still carried himself like an athlete: proud, strong, but light on his feet.

When I first saw him in person, it was a little like watching a younger Barack Obama chasing his daughters around a backyard party. He had that same calm charisma, an easy smile, and a natural affection for his girls that poured out of him without him even noticing.

His profile had already impressed me: a full-time solo dad, a passionate chef, and a man who loved his daughters like his own breath.

But seeing him in real life, it hit differently. David knew about my love for plantains, and he spoiled me. He cooked plantains in every way possible: fried, boiled, mashed, and caramelized. He sang while cooking, a beautiful, happy sound that filled the house like sunshine. Soft bachata melodies, sometimes old boleros, all sung with a voice that was more heart than technique.

There was something so peaceful, so honest, about those afternoons. At first, we kept things friendly. David was cautious. He didn't want to introduce anyone to his daughters unless he was sure. I appreciated that. He invited me over a few times just to hang out, to get a sense of each other without rushing anything. Then came his birthday party. It was a small family gathering, full of food, laughter, and little girls darting between the adults like fireflies. I met his three daughters—sweet, smart, slightly mischievous—and his whole extended family.

The girls adored their father. You could see it in the way they climbed onto his lap, how they listened for his approval, and how they smiled when he smiled. It was beautiful. It was overwhelming.

His ex-wife, I learned, was White, just like my own mother. It struck me, sharply but quietly. Life repeats itself, sometimes without permission.

I didn't ask questions about his past. I didn't need to. As women, we carry too many invisible burdens. Who was I to judge the decisions of another woman I never met? I didn't know her story. Maybe she left for reasons that made perfect sense to her. Maybe she left with a heavy heart. Maybe it wasn't a matter of love but of survival.

That night, after the party, after helping clean up the mountains of plates and sticky juice glasses and pieces of birthday cake smeared into the furniture, I drove home in silence. Something inside me shifted. I realized I was no longer the little girl watching her stepmother build a family from scratch. I was the woman being asked if she wanted to pick up that same heavy task. Except now, it wasn't a noble dream. It was real. It was messy. It was exhausting.

David was wonderful. His daughters were wonderful. But I wasn't sure that wonderful was enough. I didn't call him for several days after that. I needed the space to think, to feel, to tell myself the truth.

When I finally saw him again, I kissed him on the cheek, smiled warmly, and thanked him. It wasn't just for the plantains, or the songs, or even the affection. My gratitude was for trusting me with a piece of his life and showing me a beautiful, complicated, and honest version of family.

I told him my back story and how I had grown up believing that love could fix anything if you just worked hard enough. I shared that now, standing at the edge of my own adult choices, I realized: love needed more than hard work. It needed desire. It needed joy. It needed to feel like a choice, not a duty.

David understood. His eyes were soft and kind. He hugged me tightly, and then he let me go. A piece of my heart stayed with him and his daughters.

Not all love stories end with a kiss. Some end with a quiet blessing and a door left gently open.

For the first time, I honored my stepmother the way she deserved. And I finally related to my mother's leaving, not as abandonment, but as a human act of survival. That was my blessing, my curse, and my lesson. I had to understand the duality and forgive.

I was finally able to free myself from the story I was born into and choose the one I wanted to write.

Cultural Glimpse - The Dominican

In the Dominican Republic, love is a family recipe passed down with spice, patience, and repetition. Men are taught to provide, protect, and serve—sometimes at the cost of their own dreams. David cooked like he loved: slowly, with intention, and always for someone else. But duty is not the same as desire.

Date 20
Luca: The Perfect MapleMan for that Perfect Picture

I f either of us had changed our minds, we might've looked perfect. The picture-perfect couple. But maybe that was the problem — we were too busy looking.

There are some connections that feel like they were meant to happen in another life. Luca and I had that cinematic symmetry — like characters from parallel stories who briefly wandered into the same frame. Our timing? Almost perfect. Our chemistry? Effortless. Our conversations? Full of maybes and almosts. We were the kind of pair that would've made sense on paper. But real love doesn't happen on paper. It happens in presence, in choice, in rhythm. And neither of us quite stepped in. Maybe we were both too careful. Too curated. Waiting for the other to say the first impossible thing. Maybe we liked the idea of each other more than the reality. Or maybe, like two dancers waiting for the same cue, we never moved at the same time.

It wasn't heartbreak. It wasn't even disappointment. Just a quiet undoing of a script that never got written. Sometimes, what's picture--perfect... just never gets printed.

20 - Luca:

When I met Luca for the first time, right underneath the CN Tower on a perfect golden fall afternoon, it felt like stepping into a dream I didn't even know I had.

We had been chatting for weeks with long, thoughtful conversations, careful questions, and playful jokes. I had done everything I could to know as much about him as possible before meeting. Maybe I was being a little cautious, but he was so handsome that he looked like he belonged in a framed photo above someone's fireplace.

The first time we met, he was wearing a red-and-black plaid shirt, a toque pulled down over his dark hair, and smiling like the Canadian wilderness had personally sent him to greet me.

He was tall and broad, the kind of hunk we call in Brazil a picanha—a prime cut with just the right layer of fat. Juicy. He wasn't a gym-sculpted, six-pack type. He was a "real man's man". He had a sexy belly. This was a man you could hug and actually feel held.

I swear, as I walked toward him, I thought all of that (and more). I even laughed at myself quietly, feeling like my own teenage dreams were clapping from the bleachers.

As we talked in person, something more serious came into focus. We had little in common. I'm not talking about hobbies, music taste, or favorite foods. This was deeper: we weren't on the same page about what we wanted out of life.

Luca wasn't just looking for love. He was looking for the mother of his future child, and he wasn't shy about it. He wanted a family, and he wanted it badly—now.

I had never seen anything like it, not from a man. Where I come from, in Brazil, men often want children, too, but the social structure there still operates under some outdated laws and expectations. Under Brazilian law, even today, the child is almost always presumed to be the mother's responsibility. The weight of raising a child physically, emotionally, and financially still falls overwhelmingly on women's shoulders. Fathers can love their children deeply, but the system itself sends a clear message: the child is "hers" to raise, first and foremost. This reality, stitched into culture and law, keeps women locked into certain roles. It shapes relationships, ambitions, and even the choices women think they can or cannot make.

Here was Luca, standing under the CN Tower, offering me a whole different vision. He didn't want a woman to raise a child for him. He wanted to be a father, fully, completely, and visibly. He wanted partnership, and he wanted presence.

Ironically, life was handing me something I had long said I wished existed: A man who wanted to show up fully as a parent who didn't see childcare as her job. A man who wasn't looking for someone to disappear behind the title of "mom."

I felt a sense of panic. Luca was wonderful, but standing there with this picture-perfect man who ticked so many imaginary boxes, I realized something about myself: I wasn't ready to make that commitment. Maybe I never would be.

It's a strange feeling when your ovaries are throwing a party, but your brain refuses to leave the house. My body reacted to Luca's charm, warmth, and stability. But my soul knew if I stepped onto that path, it couldn't be halfway.

If I were going to become a mother, it had to be from a place of wholehearted "yes," not from gratitude that someone so good wanted me, not from pressure, and not from fear of missing a "perfect" opportunity.

At that moment, I realized my answer. I passed a test I didn't know life was giving me. I felt stronger, clearer, and more faithful to myself.

If I had said yes out of fear or guilt or gratitude, I would have betrayed myself and, eventually, betrayed him, too. He deserved someone whose dreams matched his dreams. I deserved to honor the quiet voice inside me that whispered: Not this way. Not right now.

Still, Luca was and is the kind of dream where I come from. Someone the patriarchy carefully planted in my brain when I was a little girl. I could see our future so clearly: Us, in some cozy house somewhere, framed photo on the mantel, and with two kids and a dog running around.

Luca made my ovaries dance, but my heart stayed stubbornly still. So, I left him with a soft goodbye. One of the greatest gifts a woman can give herself is the right to say "No." For the first time in my life, I chose to believe that I was allowed to wait for a life that fit me fully, not just one that fit me halfway.

Cultural Glimpse – The White Canadian

In Canada, love is often polite before it's passionate. Feelings are hinted at, not declared until the silence gets too loud. Luca wore irony like armor and sincerity like a secret. He wanted connection but feared the cost of being seen.

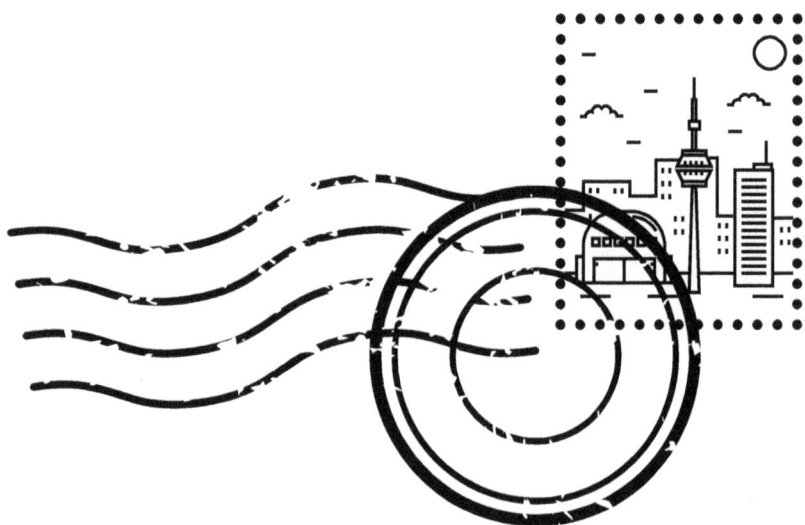

Date 21
Stephen: The Scottish McHusband

He was the man I thought I'd marry back when I was still playing with dolls.

Stephen was the dream you build as a little girl with plastic furniture and lace-trimmed fantasies. The kind of man you imagine placing beside your Barbie, right after the tea party and just before the wedding — calm, kind, and conveniently available. He was soft-spoken, Scottish, and sweet in a way that felt like a lullaby. The kind of man who rescues dogs and means it. Who says "lovely" instead of "hot," and texts back before your doubt even has a chance to settle and for a while, it felt lovely. Really lovely.

But I've always known how to wake myself from dreams. Especially the ones that are too quiet for my fire. Because being chosen doesn't mean being seen. And being adored doesn't mean being met. Stephen was beautiful in theory. A dream husband in a dollhouse life. But I had outgrown plastic rooms and soft-scripted futures. He deserved someone still playing that game.

And I? I was building something real.

21 - Stephen:

Stephen had the last name I used to give my dolls' husbands when I played pretend weddings as a little girl. You know, the dream surname that sounded both noble and cozy. The kind you could imagine printed on mailboxes, etched onto shared library cards or passed down to children with curly hair and fierce opinions. When I saw it on his dating profile, I laughed out loud. Childhood-me would have screamed. Adult-me was intrigued.

His photos were charmingly consistent: short and chubby like a teddy bear, always in a crisp shirt, and posing beside dogs or smiling in front of Scottish castles. His energy said "small-town pub" more than "highland warrior," but his words had weight and kindness. He was a serious kind of man with a glimmer in his eye that made you think he knew how to make a really good stew or fix a broken radiator without complaining once.

Stephen introduced himself like a gentleman—polite, measured, and unmistakably Scottish. His message wasn't flashy. It was warm like tea. He mentioned liking history, travel, animals, and strong women. He said something about having a deep respect for women who knew who they were. He even referenced a book I loved, which made me sit up a little straighter.

When we chatted, he came across as a businessman—the reliable kind, a grown man in all the best senses. He spoke about leadership, loyalty, and doing things properly. There was something deeply grounding in that. He wasn't selling me dreams, just offering the truth of who he was...or so I thought.

Before we met, he did something I'll never forget: he warned me about his body hair. Yep.

With endearing bravery, he messaged me to say: "Just so you're not shocked, I'm pretty hairy. Like, really hairy."

It was the first time I'd ever seen a man lead with that kind of vulnerability, and it melted me. He wasn't self-deprecating, just honest. It was oddly sexy—not the hair, but the way he owned it.

We met in person at a café that smelled of cinnamon and roasted coffee. He walked in wearing a soft wool sweater and a big grin. In person, he was even more teddy bear than I expected, warm and huggable, with a twinkle that made you feel instantly safe. His accent could've melted concrete.

He was everything I had told myself I wanted: kind, solid, emotionally available. He talked about his past with openness and his ex with respect. When he discussed his future...I was surprised.

Over a second cup of coffee, Stephen leaned in and told me he was planning to leave his business behind. "I've had enough of the corporate life," he said. "My real dream is to open a dog rescue."

I couldn't believe it. "A what?"

112

He smiled like a little boy confessing to sneaking biscuits before dinner. "A rescue. I've always wanted to do it. Just dogs. Maybe some old ones, maybe the ones nobody else wants. I've been planning it for years."

Something in me paused. I adore dogs. But suddenly, I wasn't sure what future we were talking about anymore. My mind did a quick scan of logistics: rural life, muddy boots, dog hair in every crevice. How would I visit my family? Would I have to trade airplane tickets for chew toys?

I hated how quickly practicality stole the moment. I could see the dream in his eyes. But I wasn't ready to live in a rescue center. I was still rescuing myself.

Still, we kept talking. We went for walks. We laughed a lot. I liked him. I appreciated his kindness and the way he talked about second chances, not just for dogs but for people. For a while, I imagined that maybe we could find a middle ground. Maybe I'd be the glamorous dog stepmom with frequent flyer miles.

But I wasn't ready to give up my vision of the future. I had dreams, too. I wanted to travel. I needed to hug my family every few months without having to schedule around feeding schedules and kennel hours.

I started to pull away gently. I didn't want to waste his time.

We didn't end dramatically. There was no argument or betrayal. I thanked him for being honest, for sharing his dream, and for giving me a glimpse of a kind of love that was quiet and brave. I kissed his cheek and told him that while I admired his path, mine was leading somewhere else.

We stayed in touch on Instagram. Years later, scrolling through my feed, I saw a photo of Stephen, muddy and grinning, surrounded by dogs. The rescue had opened. He had done it. I cried a little because I was proud of him for following through. He'd created a life out of care. He had saved something. In some small way, I think he saved a piece of me, too.

So, no, this isn't a love story in the traditional sense. It's a story about dreams and having the courage to share them, even if it scares people off. I learned to see people for who they are becoming and not just the current version of themselves. I also learned a lot about fur, dogs, unexpected kindnesses, and the kind of romance that leaves you better than you were at the start. And a last name that still makes me smile.

Cultural Glimpse - The Scottish

In Scotland, love hides beneath humor, and dreams are spoken quietly, if at all. Men are forged in the wind, in the whiskey, in the memory of those who came before. Stephen didn't dazzle. He steadied.

He offered not a spark but a place where I could be present and exhale.

Date 22
Carlos: The Salvadorian Almost Love

Some love stories are written in the stars. Ours was scribbled in the margins.

Carlos was the kind of man who made you believe in fate. Our paths crossed like a well-timed plot twist, filled with serendipity and shared glances that hinted at something more. He had a way of making the ordinary feel extraordinary, turning mundane moments into memories. We laughed easily, our conversations flowing like a familiar song. There was comfort in our connection, a sense that we had known each other in another life. It felt like the beginning of something significant. But sometimes, beginnings are all you get.

When silence expectations weren't meet, the spark dimmed. The conversations that once flowed effortlessly became strained. The shared glances turned into distant stares. We were two people holding onto the idea of love, rather than love itself.

Carlos taught me that not all connections are meant to last. Some are brief, beautiful interludes that remind us of what's possible. They leave us with lessons, not regrets. And so, that our love stories can be a beautiful chapter — even if not the whole book.

22 - Carlos:

Carlos and I didn't start out as a whirlwind romance. In fact, it was slow, calculated, and purely professional at first. He had been one of the many patients I'd seen at the office where I worked, but what set him apart was that he didn't fit the usual mold. Carlos wasn't loud or showy; he was quiet, humble, and had an air of mystery that made him stand out without trying. He'd often come in with his mother, a dutiful son in a world that didn't always show much gratitude for that kind of dedication. I couldn't help but notice how much he cared for her.

Carlos was the middle child of three boys, and I learned quickly that he didn't take the same direct, forceful approach his older brother had—who had tried and failed to gain my attention. But Carlos was different. After an argument with one of the doctors, he wasn't a patient anymore, and that's when he began to make his move. At first, I didn't notice, or perhaps I didn't want to. I gave him the same treatment I extended to all patients—professional, detached, polite, but nothing personal.

But Carlos wasn't convinced. For six months, he pursued me in the quietest, most skillful way. He didn't push, he didn't rush, but he made it clear that he wasn't going anywhere. Small, thoughtful gestures began to pop up: anonymous flowers, perfectly timed gifts, and an uncanny knowledge of my favorite café for a little cafecito. The more I saw these quiet but persistent efforts, the more undeniable it became. I couldn't help but admire how he had crafted his pursuit, like a scholar of love, studying every move and every moment.

Carlos had an easy charm and an effortless grace that made him seem like he was walking through life with a certain rhythm. He didn't need to boast about his abilities or his intentions. He let his actions speak for him, and with each step, he made it impossible for me to ignore him.

His family was from El Salvador, and he had a distinct Latin swagger about him. It reminded me of childhood movies where a man, with a glance or a smile, could sweep you off your feet into a dance you hadn't even known you were meant to do. It was as though Carlos had been trained in the art of making a woman feel like she was the center of his world, all while keeping his composure.

But beneath the surface, Carlos was a man of few words. His voice was low, calm, and controlled, never raising above the steady hum of his thoughts. He wasn't the type to lose himself in drama. The more I got to know him, the more I realized how grounded he was. He wasn't the flashy kind of romantic. He was the kind who would work tirelessly to give you everything you wanted, no matter the cost. He wasn't about grand gestures; he offered quiet, unwavering support.

Over time, I realized that we communicated in two languages: English and Spanish. Spanish, a language I'd learned through friends and conversations, always felt like more than just words. It was a bridge between us, an unspoken understanding that went deeper than communication.

Finally, after months of this quiet dance, I agreed to meet him. Once I did, it became clear: Carlos had won me over by showing his love for me and not simply talking about it.

We began dating without much conversation about the future or marriage or kids. It was simple—what you did when you found someone you wanted to be with. You didn't need plans; you just moved forward. I began calling him Carlos Eduardo, the same name as my childhood sweetheart, and I couldn't help but laugh at the strange twist of fate. It felt surreal, yet somehow perfectly fitting.

Carlos, raised in Toronto, was not unfamiliar with Canadian dating culture, and I assumed, like me, that he had a broader perspective on relationships, one that might have him questioning the assumptions we both grew up with. But no, much to my surprise (and I really should have known better), Carlos approached me with the same traditional mindset I had, as if we were back in Latin America. He talked about marriage and children as if they were the natural next steps, and I couldn't believe it.

We were so similar, yet so different. We were both shaped by our cultures and our roots, and here we were in a Canadian context, navigating these cultural layers in a way I hadn't expected. It was surreal, yes, but it also felt strangely comforting. In that moment, I realized I wasn't looking for a husband. I was looking for a partner who would walk beside me, not ahead of me, not behind me, but together.

Carlos had the timing of a well-placed line in a good book. The kind that shifts something in your chest. We met as if the day had waited for us. Not grand, but specific. He made the everyday shimmer—street corners, coffee spoons, late afternoon light. We laughed like we'd done it before. Conversations curled around us with ease. There was warmth, like returning to a place you didn't know you missed.

I wanted to believe we'd found something rare. And maybe we had. But timing isn't the same as compatibility. What starts with a spark still needs tending. Ours cooled before we realized the fire had gone out. The ease became effort. The lightness turned heavy. We spoke the same words, but they no longer landed.

Sometimes, you both stay longer than the connection. You try to rewrite the story instead of turning the page. It's a quiet unraveling. No betrayal. No storm. Just the slow drift of two people walking in opposite directions, still facing each other.

During our time together, Carlos changed his car—one that we had affectionately named "Darkness"—and I even managed to instill in him a love for Harry Potter, a franchise he had never been interested in. He named his puppy Luna, and every time I said her name, it reminded me of the unexpected twists our relationship had taken, like this one, to me a little marriage proposal, hidden in between the lines.

Carlos didn't give me forever. He gave me a moment that mattered. Some chapters are meant to be short. And still, they hold meaning. I carry that. I carry me. That's enough.

We laughed easily, our conversations flowing like a familiar song. There was comfort in our connection, a sense that we had known each other in another life. It felt like the beginning of something significant.

But sometimes, beginnings are all you get. When expectations weren't met, the spark dimmed. The conversations that once flowed effortlessly became strained. The shared glances turned into distant stares. We were two people holding onto the idea of love rather than love itself.

Carlos taught me that not all connections are meant to last. Some are brief, beautiful interludes that remind us of what's possible. They leave us with lessons, not regrets.

Some love stories can be a beautiful chapter, perhaps even the whole book, and some are not. And that's all that matters.

Cultural Glimpse - The Salvadoran

In El Salvador, love often whispers—humble, faithful, and folded into routine. Romance is not a performance; it's consistency. Carlos didn't chase. He stayed. And in his quiet, I heard something rare: devotion without demand.

Date 23
Rajesh: The Pakistani Diva

Some men don't seduce with touch. They seduce with theories.

Rajesh didn't arrive like a storm. He arrived like a theory about the storm. A walking lecture at the corner of Yonge and Queen, where bright lights hit broken souls and the storefronts reflect versions of ourselves we haven't met yet.

He talked like a man who read too much and felt too little. Wrapped in layers of philosophy, he made arguments sound like intimacy. "Truth," he'd say, standing near the Eaton Centre, "is only ever relative." But the way he stared made it feel like only his truth mattered. He called himself radical. A feminist, even. But his kindness had terms. His affection was a reward. His wit—a performance that only applauded itself.

There's a particular kind of manipulation that wears glasses and quotes Foucault. It doesn't scream — it outsmarts. You don't even notice the leash being fastened, because you're too busy admiring how elegantly it was braided. I should've known.

But Queen Street was glowing, and I mistook intellect for wisdom. I confused agreement with alignment. I believed that a man who spoke of revolution couldn't possibly be staging one inside my mind. He never raised his voice. He raised doubts. And those, I've learned, can be far more dangerous. Not every predator bites. Some just argue better than you can.

23 - Rajesh:

Back to the lab again. I, the accidental social scientist in hiking boots, was ready to venture into another emotional field study.

Rajesh was short and brown-skinned, with thick black hair and eyebrows so perfectly trimmed it felt like he approached grooming with surgical precision. His eyes were intelligent and deeply observant, like he could spot a thesis in a coffee stain. From the moment we started talking, I knew I was in for something different. He was smart and precise. Despite being light-years ahead of me academically, it felt like our brains were tuned to the same frequency, sometimes so finely it made me uncomfortable because it was so intimate. Intimacy, when not softened by romance, can feel like staring into a mirror with fluorescent lighting.

Rajesh was here in Canada for one of his biology PhDs. Yes, one of them. His academic track record read like a UNESCO resume. From a traditional Pakistani family, he had landed in Toronto with a brain full of evolution and a bag full of cultural expectations. When he first messaged me, I was puzzled. My biases kicked in immediately. I thought, unfairly, that men from Pakistan didn't usually date outside their culture. I assumed arranged marriage was still the dominant narrative. But instead of backing away, I leaned in. I wanted to know more. I wanted the insider version you don't get from textbooks or casual documentaries. And Pakistan, unlike India, still felt like a mystery to me. I had so many questions, and Rajesh had so many answers. Too many, perhaps.

Our early conversations were electric. He was funny, deeply articulate, and refreshingly blunt. He spoke about biology the way people talk about their first love—nerdy, poetic, and obsessive. It was infectious. Maybe because I once flirted with biology as a teenager, I understood the sparkle in his eye when he talked about frogs, ecosystems, and evolutionary loopholes. It wasn't sexy in a conventional sense, but it was undeniably captivating.

But if Carlos had treated me like his muse, Rajesh expected me to treat him like mine. He was a Don Juan of the intellect, making passionate cases for why I should "invest in him." The whole dynamic felt like I was being sold real estate in the afterlife. "Trust me," he'd say with a knowing grin. "There's long-term value here." I'd laugh, half-impressed, half-disturbed. He was the first man I'd met who openly demanded to be pursued. It wasn't confidence. It was entitlement wrapped in a scholarly samosa.

I found myself questioning things I didn't even know I had internalized. Why did I expect him to do the courting? Why did I assume the man should chase, not be chased? As someone who prided herself on feminist values, I had never challenged that part of the equation. I had never really looked at how deeply I had absorbed traditional gender roles. Rajesh was breaking the mold. I felt seen and tested all at once.

We hiked around Toronto's parks, sometimes in silence, sometimes in debate. He would pause mid-trail to explain the mating behavior of an obscure amphibian or point out the medicinal use of a plant I hadn't even noticed. His mind was a living encyclopedia, and I felt like I had front-row access to a private TED Talk. But over time, the lectures began to replace the conversations. I was no longer his date. I was an audience member.

He would vanish for days, lost in his studies. No texts. No check-ins. Just poof. Then, like a magician reentering the stage, he'd message again as if nothing had happened. "Hello," he'd say. "I've been working on a fascinating protein mutation. How have you been?" At first, it was charming, like dating someone half-prince, half-professor. But eventually, it became clear: Rajesh didn't have room for another person in his internal world. He was too busy being his own universe.

It wasn't emotional unavailability in the classic sense. It was something deeper and structural. He reminded me of a dinosaur emotionally, heavy with ancient knowledge but somehow extinct in terms of vulnerability. He knew feminism. He talked about equality. But his actions were out of sync. He was the kind of man who could define emotional labor but not offer it. He saw himself as progressive, but in practice, he reverted to control and detachment.

I started to suspect there might be some form of neurodivergence at play. His rigidity, his black-and-white thinking, his tendency to disappear and reappear without understanding how that might affect another person—it all pointed to something beyond personality quirks. I didn't diagnose, of course, but I adjusted. I softened my expectations and studied the dynamic. It felt clinical at times but also deeply human. It made me reflect on how much we expect others to "perform" relationships the way we understand them without realizing that some people live by different emotional blueprints.

Ironically, it was through Rajesh that I saw arranged marriage in a new light. I came to understand that if you're curious enough, any relationship is a journey of discovery. You don't need love at first sight. You need openness. You need structure if your heart wanders. You need grace if your partner disappears into frog protein research for four days. I began to see how arranged marriages, while often critiqued by the West, could offer a kind of stable curiosity, a framework where love is built, not fallen into.

Rajesh flipped everything for me. He showed me what equality looks like when demanded, not gifted. He didn't ask for space; he expected it. He didn't see partnership as support but as meritocracy. If I was strong enough, independent enough, and intellectual enough, then I might earn a spot in his life. I realized I didn't want to switch traditional Western gender roles—I wanted to dissolve them. I didn't want to chase or be chased. I wanted fluidity. The kind where no one needs to perform being "masculine" or "feminine." Where love isn't a prize but a shared, evolving practice.

Our story didn't last, but it made me sharper, braver, and more aware of how I show up in relationships and how others do, too.

Rajesh opened my eyes to a new cultural paradigm, to biases I didn't know I was carrying.

Isn't discovery what science is all about? Especially when the subject is yourself.

Rajesh didn't become my partner, but he became a turning point. He made me question who I thought I had to be in order to deserve love and who I was when no one was watching. After him, I no longer needed someone to chase or impress me. I needed someone who could meet me in the middle—equal, evolving, enough. Why? Because I realized that was and is me—equal, evolving, enough.

Cultural Glimpse - The Pakistani

In Pakistan, love is often arranged, but never without art. Emotion is embroidered between duty and flair, tradition, and defiance. Rajesh was brilliance wrapped in boldness. He didn't ask for permission. He expected admiration.

Date 24
Simone: The French Connection

She didn't arrive like the others. Simone was a slow burn. A whisper in a chapter I thought belonged to someone else. She appeared not in the beginning, but somewhere near the middle—quiet, poised, already written into the margins of a man's story.

But this chapter? This one is hers. In a book filled with men, it took a woman to teach me freedom. Not the kind sold in self-help quotes or Instagram captions. The kind of freedom that tastes like wine you didn't ask permission to pour. That lives in the way she said my name—not as a question, not as a claim, but as a mirror.

Toronto had never looked so cinematic. Her presence changed the lighting. She wasn't just French. She was France—the unapologetic kind. Every movement deliberate, every gaze a conversation you weren't sure you were ready to have.

It was through Simone that I realized how many of our lessons about love are handed to us by men. And how many of them are stitched with silence. It took her to show me that jealousy is a teacher, not a verdict. That sensuality can be philosophical. That a woman can open your body and your beliefs—without ever laying a finger.

Some women arrive to shake the ground. Simone arrived to remind me I had wings. She was not a chapter. She was the key. And by the time I understood that, I was already halfway changed.

24 - Simone:

After you've been wandering around the online dating world for a while, you start noticing certain familiar faces. Some profiles just hang there... frozen in time, like old cured meats in a market that nobody's bought from in years. At first, you don't know. You swipe, you dream, and you build castles in the sky. But after a while, you start recognizing them, and you realize that some people don't really want to leave. They like it here. They belong to this endless carousel.

One day, during one of those absent-minded strolls through the "market," I saw Alex again. Still smiling in that same photo. And weirdly, so was I.

Alex was part of a couple. This time, I wasn't so much interested in him. I was interested in her. Maybe it was my growing feminism, or maybe it was the seed Alex had planted before. The idea of a partnership where women are equals and agreements are real, not just tolerated.

Alex was the kind of guy who messaged women, never pushed, and... stayed. He knew who came and went, kind of like the old neighbor who's always on the porch, waving at every passing car.

Curiosity ate me alive. So, I messaged him. "Hey Alex, what's up?"

Two days later: "Hey dear, how's it going? Have you thought a little more?"

I didn't want to mislead him. I was clear. "Alex, I'm not sure I'm ready for anything serious. But... I'd like to meet your wife. If that's on the table."

I didn't even know what I was proposing. I just knew that she fascinated me.

"That was never on the table before. I'll have to ask her. I'll let you know." Weeks later, he messaged again. "Hey there! My wife and I thought long and hard about it. I wanted to make sure she felt free to answer. She said yes. She would be happy to meet you."

"Happy" felt like a door cracking open into a new world. A happier one? Maybe.

We planned for a Saturday evening. Their kids would be away. I was anxious. I had no idea what to expect. You have to understand that in Brazil, we pretend we own the people we love. Jealousy is a national sport. Flirting is our religion. Sex, even more so. We cheat, we judge, we hide, but we protect the facade. Here I was, about to walk into the arms of a woman who had thrown all of that out the window.

Part of me, the old part, thought: Maybe she's trapped or dependent or brainwashed. I'm ashamed to say that now. Those were my biases talking. When I arrived at their place, I immediately felt... calm. They weren't hiding anything.

It was a warm afternoon. Music floated perfectly through the air. Alex was an audio engineer, so MPB Musica Popular Brasileira was on point and the whole place smelled like brunch. A charcuterie table stretched across the counter, casual but elegant.

Then she walked in. And I panicked. I hadn't even thought to ask her name! She stretched out a hand and smiled: "Nice to meet you, Simone." Her French accent was like silk, wrapping around my name, my French name, the way it was meant to sound.

I almost disintegrated on the spot. Wait—her name was Simone, too?

Alex smirked before I could speak. "I thought it would be a perfect conversation starter."

We all laughed, and the ice melted completely.

Simone was breathtaking. She had voluminous black hair. She looked like a young Christiane Torloni, the Brazilian actress with unapologetic elegance but with a sharp French edge. She was beautiful and chic. No wonder Alex loved her. Hell, I loved her.

We sat and talked about Brazil, France, Italy, Greece, life, and family. She was born in France, and I could smell Paris in the way she moved.

Halfway through, Simone leaned in. "Alex tells me you have questions. How can I help you?" God, she was gracious.

I stammered, my mind racing. I managed, "Can you tell me what marriage means to you?"

She flashed a knowing smile and explained the obvious parts: partnership, trust, and shared life. Then she said, "But sex? That's something else. Sex is a sport, mon petit. A beautiful one. You practice it with someone you're good with and someone who's good with you. Alex and I are good together—and with others."

I couldn't help it. The words tumbled out of me. "But why share him?"

She looked surprised, and then she softened. "Because if I give him the freedom," she said, "then I get it too. Sex is something you share. It's not something you cage."

My heart was pounding. She was like a mirage—sensual, strong, and free. I leaned in, breathless. She kissed me, soft, deliberate, while signaling Alex with a gentle arm to wait.

Cultural Glimpse - The French

In France, sensuality is not shameful; it's philosophy. Desire is articulated and not avoided. A woman's pleasure is part of her poise. Simone didn't seduce. She invited. In her presence, I remembered that freedom doesn't require permission.

Chapter 1 - Awakening: Coexistability

There are moments in a woman's life that are thresholds, not marked by the slow, warm unfolding of knowing someone else and yourself in a way you've never dared to before. Simone was that threshold. She was not a lover in the way we usually define it. She was almost a rite of passage. She not only awakened me, she invited me back to myself.

I had been wrestling with questions about myself for a long time. What if you are not too much? What if you are enough?

After meeting Simone through her husband Alex, one day, just she and I were sitting in a café, both of us sipping a coffee, when she said, "Mon petit chou... why do you always explain yourself? Do you think he does that?"

I laughed uncomfortably. She didn't. She just looked at me in a way no man ever had. She held me without possession. She saw me without demand. She heard the version of me I hadn't spoken aloud yet. For the first time, I wondered: What would it feel like to be loved by a woman who expects nothing... but truth?

This chapter is not about sexuality, though sensuality runs through it. This is more of a reunion of self, a part of me that forgot that she never required permission to be and to want and to own her innermost desires and needs.

Simone was the woman I didn't know I was missing. I didn't need her as a partner but as a mirror. She was a woman who had chosen love on her own terms. She had redefined commitment not as containment but as conscious presence. She was able to love her husband and love herself at the same time without betrayal. She lived integration, which disarmed me.

We didn't sleep together, but we lay together—mind to mind, breath to breath, and presence to presence. She undressed me without touching me. She taught me how to worship myself through permission to feel beautiful without guilt. She helped me crave without shame, to lead without losing softness, to let go without collapsing, and to trust what I wanted, not just what I'd been told was safe. In doing so, she gave me back to myself.

For every woman who has ever felt fragmented, who has been told she must choose sexy or wise, strong or soft, free or loved, lead or be adored—these are lies. Simone is the proof, and I am the witness. A woman reuniting with herself is the most powerful love story there is.

That was Simone's gift. She never asked me to be anyone. She invited me to be all of myself. For the first time in my life, I didn't feel like too much. I was enough. You don't need to sleep with a woman to be forever changed by her.

She lit candles in rooms inside of me that had gone dark, labeled with words like "too bold," "too sensitive," "too wild," and "too soft."

I asked her, "But what do I do with all of these feelings?"

She just smiled and said, "Feel it. That's what women do. We feel. That is our strength. Our compass. Our revolution."

I didn't argue. I had crossed a threshold, and I could not go back.

This chapter is for Simone, for Th3 Black Cat in all of us. For the untamed, fully feeling, feminine, wildly wise woman inside every reader holding this book, this is your reminder:

- You are not too much...You are not too late...

- You are not a problem to be solved...

- You are not a fantasy to be controlled...

- You are a miracle in motion...

- You are the field...

- You are the fire...

- You are the researcher and the data...

- The question and the answer...

- The lover and the lesson...

- You are enough...

Simone, wherever you are—thank you for showing me what wholeness looks like when it walks into a café and doesn't apologize for taking up space. For leading me to my coexistability powers. You were Th3 Black Cat before I knew I could become her. You didn't just love me. You reminded me how to love me. And that... changed everything.

Coexistability by Nia Yara

I didn't learn coexistability in books.
I learned it in my own skin.

As a woman who carries white blood, Black blood, and Indigenous
memory,
I grew up with the weight of contradictions inside me — where one
part of me was taught to fear or erase the other. And where love — real
love — could only begin when I stopped choosing sides within myself.

Coexistability is not a theory.
It's a survival language.
It's the peace I found the day I forgave
both the one who hurt
and the ones who were hurt.
It's the soft revolution of living in my full complexity
without apology.

To coexist in this world,
I had to learn to coexist in me first.

It's not always harmony.
Sometimes it's sacred noise.
But it's mine.

And it's how I stay whole
in a world that still tries to split me.

Date 25
Maurice: The French Canadian Divorcee

There should be a medal for surviving divorce. Not a legal certificate, not a "conscious uncoupling" playlist—an actual medal. Because coming out of a marriage can be like surviving a war where both sides lost, and the battlefield is your living room. After it ends you don't go looking for love. You go looking for normal.

Maurice wasn't chasing butterflies or soulmates. He was chasing the quiet, the sanity, a the right to eat toast in peace without someone judging the brand of butter. And honestly? I respected that.

He approached me like a man who'd read all the love manuals, burned them, and decided to freestyle.

There was a tenderness in his caution. A politeness in his flirting. Like he was applying for a job he didn't quite believe existed anymore—but still brought his résumé, just in case.

And me? I was intrigued.

Because there's something wildly attractive about someone who's done the hard work of breaking apart and still shows up—creased, careful, and curious.

Maurice reminded me: love after divorce isn't about fire. It's about warmth. It's about not flinching when someone reaches for you again.

And in this quiet intermission between chapters, we found a moment of gentle applause.

25 - Maurice:

In Toronto, my circle of friends was a kaleidoscope of immigrant women, mostly Brazilian, always loud, occasionally inappropriate, and deeply loyal. We'd get together like a migrating flock of fabulous birds: fifteen of us squeezed around a table, drinking vinho verde, laughing loud enough to trigger car alarms, and dissecting the latest drama in love, visas, or taxes.

After one of those euphoric nights—a proper Brazilian gathering filled with feijoada, gossip, and unfiltered honesty—I floated out onto Dufferin like a woman in a music video. I was lip-syncing to my own playlist, hips swaying like the sidewalk was a samba parade. That's when I saw him. Or maybe... that's when he saw me.

He was tallish with reddish-blond hair. He had a warm, half-smile that hinted at secrets, but not the bad kind. Instead of looking away when he caught me mid-dance, he leaned into it. "Hola, señorita," he said, full of charm and zero accuracy.

I laughed. The classic Latin mix-up. "Portuguese," I corrected him playfully. "I'm Brazilian."

His eyes lit up. "Maurice," he said, extending a hand like we were already in a conversation.

We exchanged numbers right there. It felt surreal because the moment had a softness, like life had paused just long enough for something to begin.

Maurice worked at the post office in an administrative job, the kind that gave him just enough structure to hold his life together after the emotional hurricane of a divorce. When we met for coffee, he was honest from the start: he was still raw. Not broken, not bitter. But raw.

"Divorce," he said, stirring his espresso, "is less about ending love and more about navigating a war you didn't enlist for."

I believed him. His divorce wasn't messy in the tabloid sense, but it was emotionally violent in the way Canadian divorces can be—quietly cruel, papered in politeness, but designed for battle. The system, he told me, didn't care if you were decent. In fact, being decent made you easier to defeat.

He spoke with a kind of haunted clarity like a man who had made it out of the fire but still smelled of smoke.

And then came the sentence that floated into the air and stayed there: "I don't want children. Never did. Never will."

It wasn't harsh. It wasn't defensive. It was factual. I respected it. I wasn't desperate to become a mother. I wasn't charting ovulation cycles or looking at baby names on Pinterest. But I also wasn't ready to slam that door shut. Not yet.

What I wanted was wiggle room. A soft maybe. A margin of error in case Mother Nature got drunk and decided to surprise me.

Maurice wasn't offering that. He had locked the door, thrown away the key, and made peace with it. I admired his clarity. But deep down, I knew I needed a back door, just in case.

We kept talking, though. I liked him. He had a French Canadian warmth—emotive, generous, slightly dramatic in the best way. There was an elegance in how he held his grief. When he smiled, I could see traces of the man he must have been before the paperwork, the custody schedules, the coldness of lawyers who don't believe in nuance.

We didn't last long. But Maurice taught me something lasting. He showed me how a legal system can twist love into litigation. He let me see that even the kindest ex can become a strategic adversary.

He reminded me that compatibility isn't just attraction. It's dreams, timing, and how tightly each of you holds your keys.

Maurice wasn't for me because he was certain, and I wasn't.

Still, I'll always remember the way he caught me dancing at a red light and joined the beat without hesitation. Because sometimes, even if the music ends early, the dance was still worth it.

Cultural Glimpse — The French Canadian

In Quebec, love is bilingual, spoken with restraint and rebellion. Divorce doesn't just divide people. It disorients identities, especially for men raised to provide. Maurice carried both weariness and wonder. He wasn't looking for a partner; he was looking for peace.

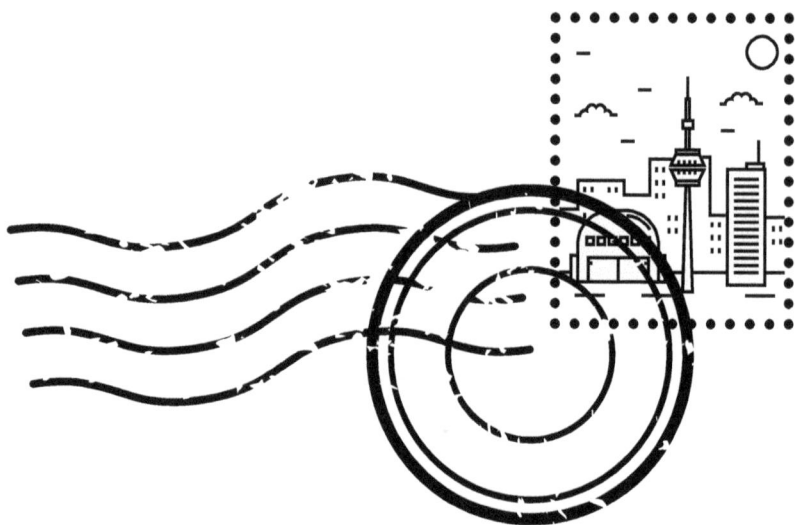

Date 26
Stephan: The Nigerian Sweet Talker

Toronto teaches you things—especially in the summer. Like how a well-cut suit on a hot day is a warning sign, not a compliment. And how charm, when wielded too smoothly, often hides something sharper underneath. Stephan messaged me in July, right when the city starts acting like it's in heat. Park dates, patios, strangers smiling at you like they already know your name. Everyone's flirting with freedom, and sometimes, with fantasy.

He called me queen before even knowing my last name. Said he'd been waiting for someone like me. The words rolled off his tongue like honey—and just as sticky. It felt good. Addictive, even. But if you've been in this city long enough, you start to recognize the difference between seduction and sincerity.

This chapter is about performance. The ones men give, and the ones we sometimes audition for, hoping the rosele comes with real affection. It's about sweet talk, fast moves, and learning how to read between the compliments.

Stephan made me feel like a goddess. Until I realized he was building an altar to himself.

Some men feel like they walked straight out of a radio station—smooth voice, perfect pitch, and a playlist of compliments ready to go. Stephan was one of those men. If charisma had a spokesperson, it would be him. He didn't just talk. He serenaded. Through texts.

He had messaged me a few times already, nothing particularly memorable at first. But one rainy Tuesday, curiosity got the better of me.

I thought, Let's see what this man really wants from a woman. If there's one group of men globally known for knowing exactly what they want—often too much of it—it's Nigerian men.

26 - Stephan:

Let me clarify before you come for me: I'm not here to stereotype. I'm here to narrate. Nigerian men have a reputation—worldwide, I might add—for being passionate, persistent, and, occasionally, persuasive to the point of performance art. A few bad apples turned into internet legends, and now, everyone walks into a conversation with a Nigerian man half-expecting to be proposed to by paragraph three.

I wasn't immune. But I was experienced.

The thing is, I grew up in a house of contrasts. My father was more military commander than romantic poet. But my Black grandfather and my cousins? Total sweet-talkers. My grandpa, bless his theatrical heart, used to incite a full-on love competition among us granddaughters.

"Whoever gives Grandpa the most kisses," he'd say, "is definitely the most beautiful."

Five girls would instantly launch themselves at him, raining kisses like confetti. To this day, we still fall over each other, fighting for his approval like we're five years old. The power of his sweet words lives rent-free in my brain.

Black men, I always say, are made of sugar-tipped tongues. If you want romance you can feel—a poetic, fairy tale, acoustic-slow-jam kind of love—call a Black man, preferably on speakerphone.

So when Stephan began texting me with his midnight radio voice and emotionally saturated monologues, I was not surprised. I was impressed. For the first few days, it felt like I was starring in a rom-com produced by Netflix Africa: big gestures, declarations of fate, emotional affirmations that came faster than Amazon Prime.

But then, just as swiftly, things started twisting.

In the same breath that he told me I was the woman of his dreams, he'd also ask why I hadn't answered his text in 23 minutes. He praised my independence but then asked if I needed so many male friends. He said he loved a strong woman, then tried to rewrite my calendar for me.

I realized something strange was happening. This wasn't courtship—it was onboarding. He was selling me a dream life, yes, but it wasn't my dream. It was his. I was supposed to move in, help manage the kids from three different women, organize his appointments, and streamline his life. I was becoming... an emotionally compensated executive assistant.

I wasn't falling in love. I was being recruited.

Still, I kept talking to him. Because it was fascinating and a little addictive. Love bombing is like sugar. You know it's not good for you, but it gives you such a rush at first. You want to believe it's real, especially when it sounds that good. He told me he wanted to build a kingdom. I didn't know I was supposed to be the castle's unpaid maintenance staff.

Eventually, we met in person. And let me tell you: the man was textbook alpha male. He was tall, confident, and smelled like a Calvin Klein commercial with an ego to match. He looked at me like I was already his. That was the biggest red flag.

Stephan didn't want to get to know me. He wanted to win me quickly, completely, and overwhelmingly. The whole experience felt like being wrapped in a designer blanket you didn't ask for—warm at first but suffocating if you stayed under too long.

But here's the twist: Stephan turned out to be one of my richest subjects. Not emotionally—God, no—but academically. I was researching love bombing at the time, and he provided hours of firsthand content. He was a walking case study. He helped me finish a full notebook and three chapters of emotional pattern theory.

So, thank you, Stephan. You didn't get the girl, but you got published—in spirit, at least.

He also taught me an important lesson that I hope other women take to heart: Love bombing isn't love. It's performance. The faster someone tries to sweep you off your feet, the more suspicious you should be. If it feels too good to be true, ask yourself whose dream you're living in.

I learned that I don't want a man who knows what to say. I want one who listens. I don't want a script. I want connection. I don't need a kingdom. I'm building my own. And if someone's offering me the moon after three conversations, chances are they're planning to hand me the invoice later.

Stephan wasn't a villain. He was a reminder that love shouldn't feel like an audition.

Cultural Glimpse - The Nigerian

In Nigeria, words are currency, and charm is a practiced craft. Men court like kings, speak like poets, and love with rhythm and spectacle. Stephan didn't just flirt. He performed devotion. But not every serenade leads to sanctuary.

Date 27
Jack: The Jamaican Poet

Toronto has a rhythm in August. It's not loud, but it pulses through Kensington, down Queen West, across the breeze on the islands. If you stand still long enough, the city hums in your bones.

That's what it felt like when Jack messaged me.

A beat. A pulse. A voice that didn't try to impress—just flowed.

He wasn't trying to be deep. He was deep. Effortlessly. Like sunlight filtered through palm trees. Like the kind of reggae you don't dance to—you sway with.

Jack was black as the midnight sea, with a voice like molasses and a smile like trouble wrapped in velvet. He wrote messages that read like verses and made my hips want to move—before we ever met.

But this chapter isn't just about seduction. It's about rhythm. The way some men speak in poetry, and live like a mixtape—equal parts Gospel, patois, and gentle chaos. It's about Caribbean charm, the dance between freedom and intimacy, and the subtle way some people make you feel like a vacation... until the return ticket quietly appears. Jack wasn't a mistake. He was music. And some songs aren't meant to be played twice.

27 - Jack:

If dating is like traveling, then meeting Jack was like stepping into a warm, tropical breeze. The kind that smells faintly of coconuts and promises you nothing but pleasure. Jack didn't enter my life. He drifted in like music from a distant speaker, unannounced, unhurried, and unforgettable.

He messaged me on a Wednesday, but it already felt like Sunday. That lazy, glowy, post-lunch kind of Sunday when time stretches and everything tastes sweeter. I could almost hear reggae in the background as I read his first words. And somehow, I started swaying, just a little, without meaning to.

Jack was short for Jackson, though "Jack" suited him better. No extra syllables. No unnecessary complications. Black as the midnight sea and just as unknowable, with a white-pearl smile that glowed against his skin like it had a halo of its own. His voice, when I finally heard it, was the sound of a poem being read over rum and candlelight.

And his walk? Mercy. Jack moved like he had no skeleton, just rhythm. Watching him cross the street was like watching a slow jam in motion. He wasn't showing off. He was simply existing—with the kind of confidence that makes your knees go, "Okay, I quit."

He didn't text like other men. He wrote in beat. Every message had cadence. Every sentence was flirtation wrapped in metaphor. They came in short, lyrical bursts that read like poetry and felt like flirting with Bob Marley's ghost. Sometimes, I'd reread them just to feel the sway return to my hips.

He told me stories of growing up by the sea, barefoot and sun-kissed. He talked about ackee and saltfish, Sunday gospel, and barefoot football games in Montego Bay. Somehow, even over a Toronto WiFi connection, I felt the salt on my skin.

I couldn't help thinking: Maybe this is what love is supposed to feel like. Not the checklists or compatibility scores. But this... soft joy. This sweet, slow thing that feels like dancing with your eyes closed in a place where no one's watching.

But Jack wasn't just a poet. He was a hustler, a visionary, and a cultural multitool. He had three phones, four businesses, and no off-switch.

He would hold me, kiss me softly, and then—mid-embrace— take a call to close a deal for a hair product line he was launching, a concert he was promoting, or an artist he was managing. I was never sure if I was dating a man or a full-fledged Caribbean enterprise.

He didn't mean to be chaotic. He simply was. Jack was a one-man carnival: part poet, part preacher, part CEO of his own beautiful mess. You didn't date Jack—you tuned into him like a radio station and hoped the signal held. And still, I liked him.

He had a way of pulling me in. I'd start to drift, and he'd sense it like a fisherman who always knew when the line was loosening. That's when he'd drop a verse. A kiss. A voice note so intimate I could feel it on my skin.

Eventually, we found a rhythm, or maybe I surrendered to his.

He started showing up on time. Turning off his phone during dinner. He'd bring coconut water in glass bottles and call it a date. I introduced him to Brazilian samba; he taught me how to slow wine in a kitchen that smelled of curry and candles. It was a cultural exchange. A sensual diplomacy. Our own little UN summit of spice, laughter, and basslines.

And the sex? It wasn't rushed. It wasn't performative. It was poetry. Erotic jazz. The kind of intimacy that made you feel like your hips had ancestors, like your thighs were writing verses.

But this wasn't a fairy tale. Jack was never going to be a husband. Not mine, not anyone's. He belonged to the world. And the world kept calling.

One day, he told me he was going to Jamaica for a few weeks—to visit family, to reconnect, maybe to stay a little longer than planned. I knew what that meant, and so did he. We didn't mourn it. We danced it. We kissed goodbye like lovers in a film noir. No tears. No explanations. Just respect.

Then, of course, came the last line: "If you ever need anything... professionally done, you know I'm one call away."

That's when the contract began. Not quite love. Not quite lust. A treaty. A rhythm. An understanding. From time to time, Jack would resurface with a message, a poem, or a question that somehow felt like a song. Once or twice... with an invitation. We'd revisit our beat and pick up our chorus with no expectations, just music.

We weren't lovers. We weren't friends. We were something that doesn't have a name in English. Maybe that's the point.

Not every story needs a conclusion. Some are melodies—beautiful, temporary, and etched in your memory like the sun after it sets.

They say, "Once you go Black, you never go back." Maybe.

But here's what I know: Once you go Jack... you never forget the rhythm.

Cultural Glimpse - The Jamaican

In Jamaica, rhythm is a birthright, spoken in patois and pulsed in flirtation. Love isn't whispered. It's sung, teased, and tasted like ripe mango. Jack kissed like he was writing a verse. He didn't promise forever. He offered vibes.

Date 28
Osmani: The Cuban Revolutionary of Love

Some men seduce you with poetry. Osmani seduced with percussion. Every word was a beat, every touch a syncopation. He didn't walk — he swayed, like he had a permanent salsa rhythm in his hips.

We met after a Brazilian party, which felt like a setup from the universe. His charm was effortless, tropical, and just dangerous enough to be delicious. He spoke like he was still on a Havana rooftop, drink in hand, world at his feet.

Osmani was short, smooth, and venomous — the good kind. The kind that makes you forget rules and remember thighs. His game wasn't subtle, but it was artful. He wasn't searching for love; he was staging revolutions — one bedroom at a time.

He flirted with waitresses. Promised domestic bliss. Smelled like rum and revolution. Sex was his uprising, and his body, a political act. I wasn't fooled. But I did play. And when I finally surrendered, it was like signing a devil's deal with a cigar.

He didn't call. Not right away. But when he did — months later, like nothing had passed — I smiled. Some men you love. Others you remember like a summer storm. Osmani was thunder with hips.

28 - Osmani:

Osmani arrived like the final trumpet in a bolero—bold, rhythmic, impossible to ignore.

He didn't walk. He strolled, as if Havana's Malecon breeze had followed him all the way to Toronto and was pushing him gently forward, hips first. He was short, sun-kissed, agile, and carried himself like someone who'd survived revolutions with nothing but a smile and cologne.

Dios mío, that cologne announced him five steps before he appeared, lingering like a good rum on your tongue.

There are many kinds of Cubans. The ones who stayed. The ones who left. The ones who stayed but had to become someone else. And then there's Osmani: the ones who never really arrived anywhere because their entire being lives in performance of charm, survival, and seduction.

We met through a friend at a Latin dance bar, one of those nights when Toronto felt like a warm bath of cultures. I was coming off a long string of complicated dates, each man a different kind of puzzle. But Osmani wasn't a puzzle. He was a game. And I knew the rules.

My father once told me, "Never play with fire if you don't know how to dance with smoke."

That night, the music was rumba, but Osmani was pure guaguancó. We danced. Of course, we did. His body spoke a dialect I'd known since childhood. He had hips that said, "I see you." His hands never grabbed but always hovered, inviting you to fall under without ever pushing.

He didn't ask what I did for a living. He didn't want my résumé. He wanted my rhythm. And I gave it to him—in small doses.

Being Brazilian, I've seen seduction used as both currency and camouflage. In Cuba, it's survival. Ask any Cuban woman who's lived through the 90s' "Periodo Especial" what it means to feed a family with nothing but black beans, ration books, and a body that could dance.

But I also knew that Cuba is not to be pitied. It is to be understood.

Tourists love to talk about how "safe" Cuba is. And it's true. You can walk through the streets of Havana at midnight with gold earrings and a miniskirt and no one will bother you. Not because they're afraid of the law but because the law of the street is older and sacred. The people are poor, yes. But their dignity is intact.

Cuba is safe for tourists because the people have made it so. Even when the government took everything, they kept their manners. But behind that safety lives something more complicated. Sex tourism. Emotional tourism. A whole system of exchange where smiles are bartered and affection can become a profession. And Osmani was a master of the system.

He told me he once worked at a resort, an all-inclusive fantasyland where North Americans go to forget their cold marriages and colder winters. He used to teach salsa by day and something far more intimate by night.

"I gave them what they wanted," he said.

"And what did they want?" I asked.

"To feel beautiful," he replied.

That stuck with me because that was what he gave me, too. Beauty.

Osmani was the kind of man who could say your name in a way that made it sound like poetry, even if you were yelling it across Dundas Street in traffic. I knew he wasn't mine. Not even for the night. He belonged to the art of the moment, to flirtation as resistance, to the ritual of pleasure not as sin but as strategy.

When we finally fell into bed, it was like slipping into a carefully choreographed play written by Celia Cruz, directed by Pedro Almodóvar, and produced by Che Guevara's ghost.

Che spoke of revolution as the "tender feeling of love." Osmani embodied that idea. Every kiss was a protest against scarcity. Every caress was a manifesto. He wasn't trying to conquer me. He was trying to survive, and bringing me pleasure was part of his gospel. It was the most professional sex I've ever had—not mechanical, not cold, but studied and executed with elegance. It was as if I were being worshipped in a temple built of heat and memory.

After, he didn't vanish. Not right away. He lingered. Lit a candle. Played music. He read me a Pablo Neruda poem from his phone. Then he kissed my shoulder and said, "You'll think of me when it snows."

He was right. We didn't date. We didn't text daily. But every few weeks, his name would appear again like a song I hadn't played in a while, now calling me back. Sometimes, I said yes. I wasn't in love. I wanted to feel alive in a language I didn't need to translate.

Osmani was not a mistake. He was an experience; a postcard from a country that taught me joy could be political and sex could be sacred. He reminded me that I didn't always need a future plan. Sometimes, I just needed a present tense. To be touched like I was still worth poetry. To laugh in a way that echoed down the block. To dance like I still believed in magic.

And so I say: thank you, Osmani. Thank you for the revolution.

Cultural Glimpse - The Cuban

In Cuba, seduction is survival, and charm is political. Men like Os-mani move like music: bold, unhurried, unforgettable. He touched like he was rewriting history. With him, every kiss felt like resistance wra-pped in rhythm.

Date 29
Darius: The Persian D-Pic Guy

If fairy tales were rewritten for the digital age, Darius would be the misunderstood anti-prince. He believed romance should arrive attached to a jpeg. He was, in essence, the reverse Rapunzel. Instead of lowering his hair from the tower, he threw his dick out the window—metaphorically and quite literally. But no one was climbing up to save him. No braid to ascend, no magic to be found. Just a lonely tower, some Wi-Fi, and a camera roll full of hopeful lighting. Maybe that's what got me—the loneliness behind the lens.

No man who feels seen starts conversations with his genitals. He wasn't a predator. He was a projection of confusion, culture, and a generation trained to click before it speaks. What he thought was seduction was really a digital SOS. Swipe-right modernity. Swipe-left intimacy.

So no—I didn't report him. I met him and I asked him the question that every woman receiving unsolicited anatomy wants to ask: What are you really trying to show me?

This is not a tale of revenge.

It's a story of curiosity. Of meeting a man not to shame him, but to understand him.

Of turning the pixel into a person.

Of holding up a mirror, not a pitchfork.

Because sometimes, the boldest thing you can do... is knock on the tower door.

29 - Darius:

Darius was that guy—the one whose camera roll is a shrine to his own dick. But Darius did something unexpected. He talked to me before sending the goods. He said this usually didn't happen—he would drop the dick-pic and disappear into the cloud. Apparently, I was special.

I'm not going to lie—it was a dick that could've made Alexander the Great raise a white flag. I was stunned...and, reluctantly, curious.

He had a face to match. Mixed-race, maybe. His skin was the color of expensive coffee, and his jawline came with its own shadow. The kind of guy who looked like he'd just woken up from a dream he wrote himself into.

His voice, when we spoke, was casual, like a whisper between sins. Then, out of nowhere, he started quoting Arabian Nights. He was a poetic pervert. I didn't know whether to block him or fall in love.

I told myself I wanted to meet the man. But let's be honest: I wanted to meet the sender of the "sacred image." The pixel priest of penis.

It wasn't just attraction. I was thrilled to meet him. The very idea of sitting across from the man who had so casually violated the digital intimacy of who-knows-how-many women sent a current through me.

I wanted to look him in the eyes. I wanted to tell him what it meant to receive that kind of unsolicited energy. I wanted him to know what it felt like to be reduced to a potential receptor. A hole, a click, a reaction. I wanted to meet him so I could tell him to his face how despicable it was.

I didn't just want to meet the man. I wanted to show him me, a real woman, and an actual person behind the screen. In a way, I wanted to represent every woman who has ever opened her phone to find a cock she didn't ask for.

It became my mission: to change one mind. We tried to meet and booked a last-minute date, but he canceled because he had an emergency.

I gave him a pass. Shit happens. The second time he canceled, he claimed a flat tire. Sure. Meanwhile, he kept coming back, sliding into my DMs with the ease of a man who knew he still had my attention. He'd pick up right where he left off—talking in double entendres, moaning in voice notes, and wanting virtual sex.

But I didn't give in. Something eventually unsettled him and he finally confessed. He admitted he didn't really want to meet up because, "It's hard to face people after they've seen you that way."

He said his face and dick were "everywhere," and most women didn't take him seriously anymore. "This is my rebellion," he said. "It's my own way of rejecting the superficiality of dating apps." He went on to claim no one was real and that no one was looking for anything true.

So he did the worst thing he could do and started fires everywhere, burning bridges before they were built. He called it honesty, but it felt more like gasoline.

It didn't take long for me to realize that he was ashamed about what he'd done. He knew what he had done was a violation, a form of digital molestation. No wonder he couldn't face the women he'd sent them to.

Suddenly, I could only see him as a case study in something larger. This wasn't just about Darius anymore. It was a snapshot into the world of entitlement, disconnection, and the strange shadow-side of our digital lives.

Darius, disconnected and entitled as if someone owed him something, thought he was rebelling against superficiality. But in doing so, he became the very thing he claimed to resist. He became just another man looking for something real by acting unreal.

I don't know if I changed his mind. We never did meet. Eventually, the thread went cold, like a fire with no wood left to burn. But I'd like to think something stayed with him. Maybe the echo of my voice, or the quiet way I didn't give him what he wanted, or maybe the mirror I held up.

Hopefully, he realized that the thrill he was chasing was not nearly as powerful as the truth I was holding.

Cultural Glimpse - The Persian

In Persian culture, poetry and pride walk hand in hand. Men are raised on Rumi, but some forget the soul behind the verse. Darius sent pixels, not presence. But behind the bravado, I sensed a boy mistaking rebellion for romance.

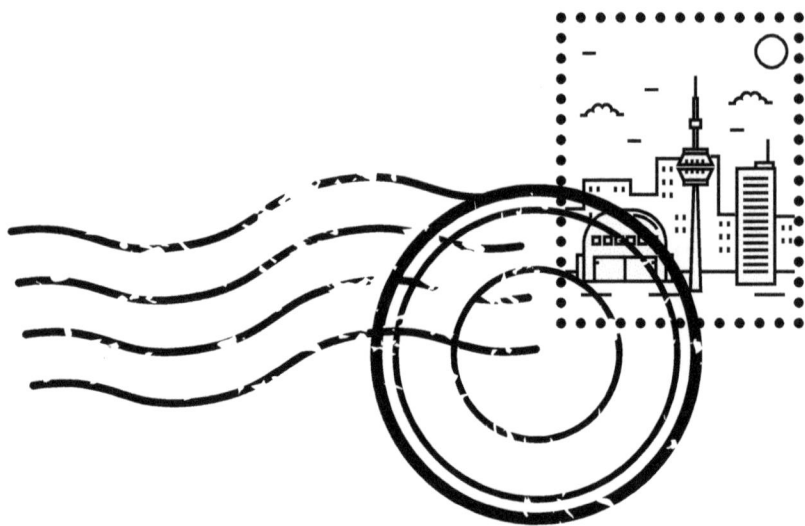

Date 30
Adrian: The Romanian Spell

I immigrated to Canada as a professional firefighter, so safety wasn't just a slogan, especially not in bed. Condoms were non-negotiable. If you want to enter my body, and I have no idea where you've been, you'll wear a condom—end of story.

Because of safety, I used to book my dates around the Danforth, which was close enough to the subway, where it would be hard to follow. I even had a few places where I was discreetly recognized for bringing my dates. But it kept me safe. Some of those spots had a double entrance, a quiet little escape route in case things went sideways. Safety first.

Despite all that planning and precautions, I wasn't immune to being deceived. No one is. You can know the exits, carry the condoms, trust your instincts, and still miss the part where someone's charm is a script. Safety protects your body. But the heart? That's another battlefield—one where even seasoned woman sometimes forgets the oldest rule: not every man who looks at you like a mystery wants to solve gently.

30 - Adrian:

One rainy evening, I got a message. My nickname on the app was Th3 Black Cat. It was a special pickup line. Adrian finally cracked it in that first message.

Adrian was average-looking and not the typical eye candy I had gotten used to. But he had something undeniably sexy to me, something I hadn't known I desired until that moment: a huge, beautiful nose.

151

Yes. I know. Don't judge. We like what we like. I was magnetized. That nose, that clever line referencing Th3 Black Cat—and then he messaged again with a Spider-Man quote. My heart skipped. I was smitten.

From then on, I studied him, his history, his culture, and his language. I became a student of Adrian. He spoke Romanian with a touch of Spanish, and we exchanged love words in all three languages—English, Spanish, and his native tongue. It was intoxicating.

It was a new kind of love I hadn't known existed. I submitted, not out of weakness but out of surrender. I wanted to be his woman... whatever the hell that meant to him.

We told each other everything. It felt like two ancient souls reuniting. Even now, I wonder if he was real. He felt made for me.

Maybe because... he was made up. From the first hug, I felt like I fit into him. He made me question everything I thought I wanted. Maybe I did like guys a little ugly. Maybe I was Camilla, and he was my Gonzo. I didn't care.

My life was full. I had performances and presentations, and I did pole dance at a studio in Toronto. I was busy, life was booming, and maybe because of that, I didn't notice we weren't meeting as often anymore.

That's the thing about being easygoing. The wrong ones sniff it out. I was too involved to realize until it was far too late. He was married.

I can't tell you he lied. I've reread our conversations. He never said he was single. It wasn't like the manipulative Alex situation. But it shattered me. I was muted, shaken, and hollowed out.

The loudest sound I ever heard was the silence after he shattered me. It wasn't a scream or a sob; it was the sound of everything stopping at once, then trust hitting the floor and breaking in places no one could see.

Once the noise of heartbreak faded, I saw it all—the structure of the lie, the choreography of his seduction, and the woman on the other side of his life. She wasn't my enemy. She was my sister. She was another woman manipulated by the same man.

I did what every sane and rational woman does when she reaches that realization: I investigated. And my Brazilian girlfriends—forget the FBI; those women could find your mother's maiden name with just your shoe size. They found it all: his wife, his children, and even his address.

I debated for weeks, and then I messaged her. It was short. Hello, and I'm sorry. I have a story to tell you, and I wish we can talk. This is my number. The ball is in your court. I accept and respect any decision you make.

With that, I closed the chapter on Adrian. Loyalty to women must always come before loyalty to the man who betrays them both. Sisterhood begins when we believe each other. And the only antidote to being silenced is to speak.

When women protect one another, the patriarchy doesn't stand a chance.

Cultural Glimpse - The Romanian

In Romania, sweetness hides in stories, in glances, and in golden dessert wine. Men speak in riddles and seduce like folklore—velvety, mysterious, slow to reveal. Adrian poured words like Tokaji: rich, ancient, intoxicating. But not all sweetness, is safe to swallow.

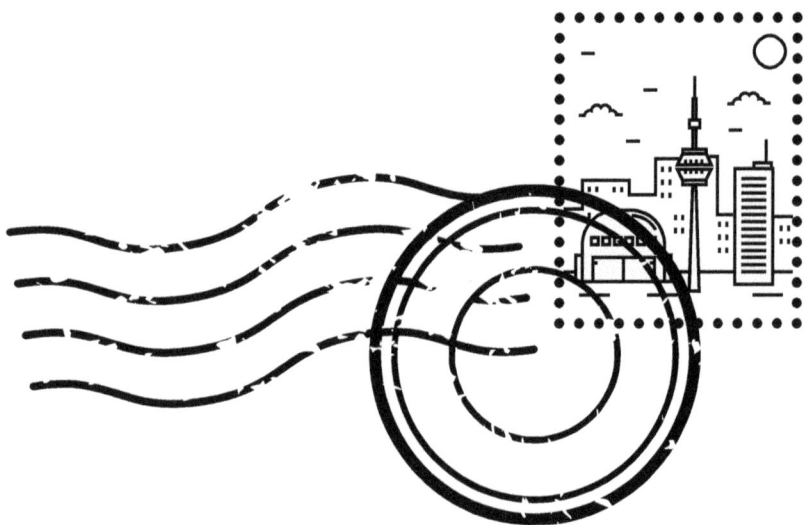

Date 31
Aoi: The Japanese Ritualist

oi didn't collect women. He curated encounters.
A chemist by day and sensory mystic by night, Aoi
had one rule when he traveled: one woman per country.
One story. One offering. A ritual, not a romance. He
wasn't chasing bodies—he was composing a sensual encyclopedia, one
country at a time. He hadn't been to Brazil yet—but this was Toronto.
The whole world passes through here.

When he invited me for a massage, it wasn't a pickup line. It was
a ceremony. His home smelled of cedar and matcha. He handed me a
silk robe like a sacred uniform. There was a mat on the floor, soft lighting, and no rush. Aoi didn't undress me. He unveiled me—layer by
layer, cell by cell. It wasn't about sex. It was about memory. Permission.
Knowing.

He never crossed a line because there was no line—only the space I
gave him. The respect made it hotter. That night, I didn't come. I arrived. And when I left, I felt like a chapter worth rereading. A mystery.
A Mona Lisa. A whole country. Aoi didn't want to keep me. He just
wanted to understand me—fully, fleetingly, and with care. And that is
also a happy ending.

31 - Aoi:

After a long hiatus of getting my life back in order and doing therapy twice a week for months, I finally recovered but not unharmed. I
lost my nose in the battle—pun intended.

But I regrouped. I decided to come up with a simple, honest plan. I needed something feminine and structured, something that made sense to my healed and practical heart.

That's when my Five Feminine Pillars (FFP) were born. There were my minimums.

- Open to either having or not having kids

- Family-oriented

- Educated

- No vices

- No snoring

I chose one physical trait, and I stand by it. Minimalist structure means five is the limit, and after ending a relationship with a man who snored, I realized how much it bothered my ex-firefighter, light-sleeper self. I had never felt so rested. It was like my nervous system finally had a break. No more snoring. It was a non-negotiable.

I felt these rules were fair. I was now armed to my core with resolution and healed from my wounds. I marched again. Avante, companheiras!

I must've whispered this to my future self. Back then, there was no book idea. Just me, a little stronger, a little wiser, and ready to flirt again with the world.

Then came Aoi—a soft, blue whisper of a name. Jeff was his Western name. I laughed when he said Jefferson was "easier" than Aoi. Aoi was lighter and sweeter. But maybe, like most men, he had his own reasons for hiding softness behind practicality. Maybe it was his way of being rebellious.

Aoi's first message to me felt like origami. It was a perfectly folded note, crafted with precision and intention. It was so artful I nearly thought it was a mistake like someone had accidentally sent me a love letter meant for someone else. But it was for me. It was the kind of message that made you slow down your scroll.

Aoi was a chemist who had immigrated from Japan to Canada in his teens. Fully adapted to life in Toronto, he still preserved his roots in the most reverent ways. He lived, ate, moved, and breathed with the grace of tradition. His apartment was a peaceful sanctuary in the chaos of downtown, a slice of Kyoto tucked behind a red-brick exterior.

Toronto is a hard city; fast, cold, and ironic. I always joke that dating here feels like trying to grow orchids in asphalt. But Aoi was different. He was the little patch of moss between the cracks that thrived quietly.

I didn't even know how to reply to such a delicate man. He spoke of art, flowers, and sunsets. He told me Ontario had the best sunsets in the world, which I had never taken time to notice.

The relationship was not sexual and not non-sexual either. He was the healing balm my soul didn't know it needed. He listened to my stories about Brazil-Japan cultural ties like they were prime-time soap operas. He'd ask about food, holidays, and family values. He once stopped me midsentence to say, "You're not telling me stories. You're opening doors."

Then came the most indecent proposal ever. "I want to massage you." He said it softly and respectfully, like a question written in calligraphy.

But this wasn't flirtation. Aoi was a true collector. He traveled for work and, in every country, chose one woman to gift a massage. It was his ritual. He wasn't flashy or overconfident about it. There was no sales pitch, just a quiet pride. "I've never given a massage to a Brazilian woman," he confessed. "I think I've been waiting for you." He promised it would be the best massage of my life.

I laughed at first, then I considered it, then I said yes.

He wasn't flirty. He was respectful to a fault. I think his silence was the secret to his success. That, and the hands of a man who understood worship better than seduction.

When I arrived, he gifted me a beautiful silk robe folded in layers. I still have it. I wear it when I need to remind myself who the hell I am. It's a cape for my inner goddess.

His apartment was set up like a temple with low lighting, natural oils, and soft incense. He had a room just for it, what I now lovingly call a "massage chamber." On the floor was a warm, inviting mat.

He instructed me with the calm of a monk. Everything in me said "release," and I did. The massage was not sexual. But it was the most intimate experience I've had in a long time.

He didn't try to own me. He didn't try to impress me. He just offered, fully and generously. His touch didn't ask; it listened. That night, I remembered who I was and had always been—before heartbreak, before strategy, and before men who didn't know what to do with me.

Every time I need to recover myself, I get a massage. It's my prayer to him, the goddess he revived, and the collector who knew better than to possess.

I have never looked at Japanese men the same way again.

Cultural Glimpse - The Japanese

In Japan, intimacy is ceremony—measured, mindful, and deeply felt in silence. Touch is not casual; it is sacred choreography. Aoi moved like a monk, loved like a healer, and vanished like a haiku. He didn't need to possess me. He helped me remember myself.

Date 32
Rakesh: The Indian In-Between

It was that quiet slice of time — after the storm, before the plot twist. I had started healing, but I wasn't whole. Toronto, in its usual fashion, kept breathing around me like an indifferent lover. Streetcars rattled by. People hustled. Life, persistent and unbothered, marched on.

That's when I met Rakesh.

He was selling saris at a yoga festival on Toronto Island. A friend dragged me there, hoping incense and headstands could do what therapy hadn't. Rakesh was soft-spoken, dressed in linen, with eyes that looked ancient and amused. He spoke about yoga, past lives, and the stars like someone who knew them personally. He offered me chai. Then stories. Then perspective.

He told me about his love—impossible, blue-eyed, forbidden. His future was already arranged, a wife waiting back home, her name written in family tradition. He said it like a confession and a blessing. He didn't want anything from me. That was the gift. With him, I remembered that intimacy doesn't need to climax to matter. Some people enter your life like prayer—brief, sacred, and transformative.

Rakesh wasn't a chapter. He was a footnote in the language of healing. And Toronto, that day, felt like a quiet temple.

32 - Rakesh:

Rakesh was the kind of Indian man who looked both ancient and young at once, as if time was folding itself neatly around him like a perfectly pressed sari. Maybe it was the yoga. I'd been practicing it for years by then, but on him, it showed. He carried the softness of a monk with the presence of a warrior.

We met at my very first yoga festival, held on the Toronto Islands. It was a tiny, floating paradise with just enough wind to make the prayer flags dance and enough silence between the chanting to make your thoughts feel welcome again. I was healing, freshly rebuilt. My spirit was like a bone just out of a cast—stronger but sensitive to the touch.

He was there with his family, selling saris. Their booth was a burst of color with deep violets, marigolds, jade, and magenta. I was with a Pakistani friend who took the lead, trying on fabrics for an upcoming wedding. I was just watching, amused, letting myself be light.

Then Rakesh turned to me and insisted I try one on too. I laughed. I told him I had nowhere to wear one, but he didn't care.

He said, "You don't need a reason to feel beautiful."

How could I argue with that? Trying on a sari is almost a bit of a ritual, a slow, reverent wrapping of cloth and intention. When I looked at myself in the mirror, I saw something uncanny, like the women in the Brazilian soap operas I'd grown up watching. I looked proud, elegant, and strong. I didn't wear the sari; it wore me. And I let it.

My friend bought her dress to be picked up after alterations at their shop in Little India. Rakesh asked for my number, offering to take me for butter chicken the day we'd collect it. I said yes. Of course, I did.

He texted right away like we were old friends remembering the path back to each other.

We spoke about everything: yoga, horoscopes, rebirth, meditation. There was no such thing as an inappropriate subject with him. Every conversation felt like a window opening. There was no extraneous noise, just air and meaning.

And then, one day, he told me he was going to be married soon. It was arranged. There was no bitterness in how he said it. It was like a boulder he'd been carrying for years and could finally lay down at someone else's feet. "But I'm in love with someone else," he added. "A white girl. Blue eyes. She loves me, too."

My heart broke quietly. He wasn't fighting his fate; he was folding into it. I knew from the way he told the story that the love was real and fully realized but unlivable. We sat with that truth together. Two people who had never kissed or touched, and yet somehow shared the intimacy of loss.

I told him about Adrian and my own heartbreak. Rakesh, in his calm, yogi way, offered something unexpected. "Maybe he loved you too. In his own way."

His words reached a part of me that therapy hadn't touched. Maybe that was true. Maybe Adrian had loved me—not with integrity or longevity, but with the only language he had. That didn't make it enough... but it made it something.

Rakesh didn't try to fix me. He didn't try to save me. He was simply present with the gentleness of someone who'd been cracked open, too.

Our entire connection happened in the liminal spaces: yoga mats, sidewalks, sari shops, and text messages. But in a strange way, he healed me more than lovers did. He reminded me of perspective. Sometimes, love is not what we get but what we witness. It's possible to hold space for someone else's longing and be transformed by it. Heartbreak doesn't always need a villain or a sequel. And all of that is more than okay; it's enough.

Cultural Glimpse - The Indian

In India, love wears many forms: arranged, cosmic, devotional, and delayed. Desire is wrapped in tradition, but longing finds its own path. Rakesh spoke softly, like someone who'd made peace with not being chosen. He offered no pursuit, only perspective.

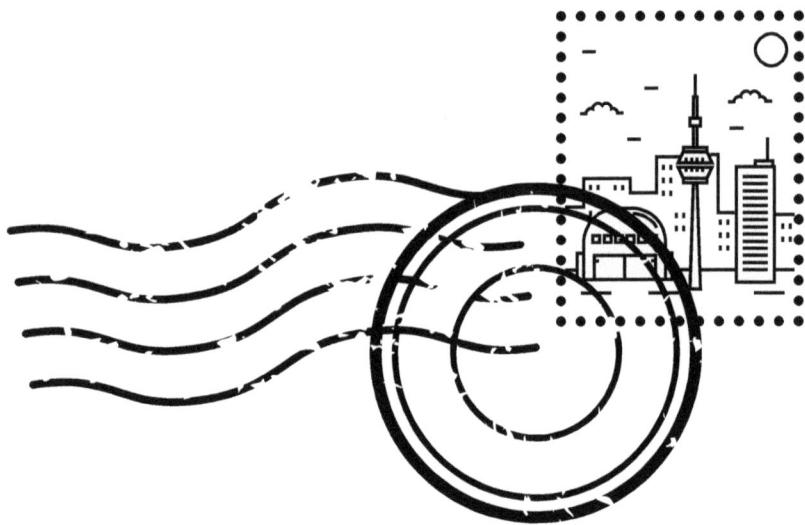

Date 33
Marx: The Native Signal

He didn't look real. Bald, blue-eyed, brown-skinned, his photo stopped me cold. Something about him felt familiar, but not from this life. I messaged him back. He answered in broken Portuguese, then Spanglish. I laughed.

Marx was Indigenous Brazilian and Ecuadorian, a son of two worlds that didn't speak the same language but somehow birthed him. His parents were still together. He inhaled rapé, worked with plant medicine, and whispered in Tupi-Guarani.

We met a few times before he moved to Vancouver to work in psychedelic research. His messages were sparse. His presence was unforgettable. Around him, I slowed down. My blood remembered its roots. My hair curled softer. Even the city seemed to quiet. He never tried to conquer me. He didn't need to. Marx wasn't a man. He was a mirror. A reminder. A walking invitation to remember my ancestors.

He didn't offer romance. He offered return. And somewhere in me, the panther purred.

33 - Marx:

We met online. His photo was... hypnotic. He had a bald head and intense blue eyes. But there was something else in his skin tone, his posture, and the way he held his gaze. He looked like a native spirit trapped in a Berlin DJ. Or maybe a Berlin DJ who got lost in the Amazon and never came back.

He was tan like a Brazilian but didn't look Brazilian. And yet, I felt like I already knew him. It was like we'd sat around a fire together in a dream. Or maybe he just had one of those faces.

163

His first message was, "Brasileira! Nem vou mandar mensagem porque você vai ignorar."

"Brazilian! I'm not even going to message you because you will ignore me.".

I laughed out loud. He said that he wouldn't send me a message because I would ignore him. Yet, he messaged me anyway. It felt so cocky that I had to respond immediately.

I messaged back: "Tenta a sorte." Try your luck.

He answered in hilariously broken Spanglish. It was a grammatical crime scene, and I was charmed.

He said he was Brazilian but from Ecuador. I said that wasn't how countries worked, but he explained his mother was White from Ecuador, and his father was Indigenous Brazilian. They met while she was doing some kind of research in the Amazon. Of course they did.

He told me I was going to be his. Then quickly added, "It's an invitation. Eternal."

I should've been terrified. Instead, I wrote down his name: Marx. I still don't know if it was his name, a statement, or a joke. Maybe it was all three.

We met in person a few times before he moved to Vancouver full-time. Our meetings were good for my spirit. He told me he was working with researchers and Indigenous elders on the therapeutic uses of Ayahuasca and DMT. "My job," he said, "is to remember."

I didn't know what that meant at first. We talked about plant medicine, the arrogance of modern science, and what gets lost when a culture forgets to listen to its grandmothers. He told me about rapé, the sacred tobacco powder that clears energy, sinuses, and sometimes your entire worldview. He used it the way some people use essential oils: with reverence, ritual, and slightly too often.

He wasn't particularly talkative, but when he spoke, it felt like bark peeling back from a tree—gentle, necessary, and slow. His words had a kind of natural rhythm and flow.

My instinct, of course, was to ruin that by talking too much. Luckily, he didn't seem to mind.

He told me I didn't know enough about my own country. He said the Brazil I was raised in had erased its roots like bad pencil marks, and the cures we still haven't found are sitting in the stories we stopped telling.

I didn't argue because he was right.

He never said he wasn't Indigenous enough to belong to his father's side nor that he wasn't White enough to belong to his mother's. But I knew, belonging was a fluid word in our world.

There was a loneliness about him, but it wasn't desperate. It was the kind of solitude that grows in old souls. He had a rare quality like he wasn't seeking love, just honoring it when it passed by. And I felt honored.

We weren't lovers, not officially or physically. But if I had a category called "the ones who changed me," Marx would get a full chapter. This one.

He told me he worked with people going through spiritual crises. His philosophy was that DMT sometimes showed people what religion couldn't and the Earth isn't something we walk on but something that walks with us. He didn't have a therapist smile or a guru tone but a matter-of-fact softness.

Soon, he told me he was leaving for good, and Vancouver was calling. "I need to be near the mountains," he said.

We're still friends to this day and text occasionally. He reminds me that not all Indigenous people live in the past. Some live in cities, in labs, and even in silence.

Cultural Glimpse - The Indigenous (Brazilian-Ecuadorian)

In Indigenous cultures, love is ancestral, spoken through silence, land, and breath. Marx didn't chase. He listened to plants, pain, and memory passed through blood. He wasn't romance. He was remembrance.

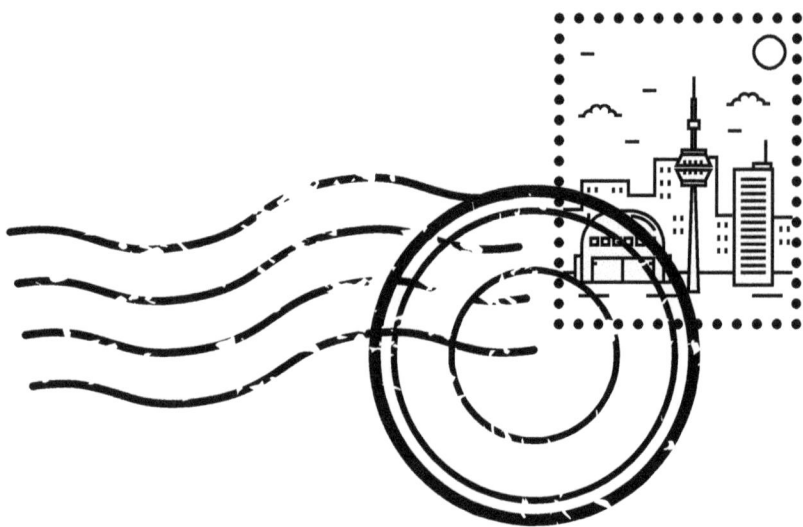

Date 34
Victor: The Argentinian Hermano, Pero no Mucho

Victor looked like bad decisions dipped in cologne. Tall, pale, with piercing blue eyes and the confident strut of a man who had never been told no. He wore an Argentine football jersey in his profile photo — a red flag to any self-respecting Brazilian woman. And yet, I swiped right.

He had that classic South American swagger, the kind that promises fireworks and emotional whiplash. Our conversations were sharp and flirtatious, full of teasing and taunts — like tango with words. But underneath the charm was a strange need to dominate every interaction. Victor didn't speak with women, he spoke at them. Everything was a test. A push. A pull.

One day, he asked if I would cook for him. I told him I wasn't the kitchen type — unless we were dancing in it. He didn't laugh. He simply said, "Women like you don't last."

Maybe not. But we burn bright.

Victor taught me that old-school masculinity, no matter how well-dressed, is still an expired script. And some of us are just here to write new stories.In the end, it wasn't a heartbreak.

It was a quiet revolution.

34 - Victor:

Victor looked like a bad decision. He had white, pale skin that almost glowed under Toronto streetlights, with dark tousled hair and piercing blue eyes that stared too directly. He had the kind of eyes you

167

regret—but only later. He had a devilish air, like Damon Salvatore from The Vampire Diaries, if Damon ever put on cologne and tried to act like a gentleman. I was all in for the looks this time. Who said a bad choice can't also be the right one for the right kind of story?

I first spotted him online, wearing an Argentinian jersey in his profile. Supporting Argentinian football in São Paulo is like being a Bayern Munich fan in Germany or a Man U supporter in England—but with more drama, more samba, and more tears. Football isn't just football for us; it's life and death. And Victor was dressed as the enemy.

I paused, but then I thought: Toronto is neutral ground, isn't it? What's the harm in mingling with the enemy? Brazil and Argentina brought together by fate, coffee dates, and algorithmic swipes.

Victor didn't hide his masculinity. I'll use that term loosely here. Looking back, it wasn't masculinity so much as an uncivilized charm——a caveman with cologne. But I've never been one to shy away from a challenge. He sounded like something I'd have for breakfast.

He was doing his version of an acasalamento dance—or an animal mating ritual, for lack of a better word. He was all swagger and testosterone, and I observed like an amused anthropologist at a wildlife reserve. The performance was so obvious that I had to call it out. That, of course, became the game. I'd twist his machismo back onto itself with a little feminist flair. Reverse psychology meets Latin flirtation. He postured, and I parried. We both kept score, like Brazil vs. Argentina.

Our first date came. Victor wanted to pick me up. It was textbook Latin romance, and I let him. He arrived with a single Hungarian rose in the passenger seat. It was delicate and almost theatrical. At my feet, nestled like a sleeping dog, was a strategically placed baseball bat. When I raised an eyebrow, he pulled it out like a knight unsheathing a sword.

"It's just in case anyone messes with you," he said, dead serious. "I'll protect you."

Don't get me wrong. Some women dream of this—a man who shows up like a knight, ready to fight dragons or ex-boyfriends or stray subway creeps. But not me. I'd rather not need protection like that in the first place. Why would I need it? Was I supposed to fear other men or men like him?

Victor lived in a world of Alpha fantasies, where danger is a plot point, and women are treasures needing guards. It wasn't his fault; he was built or programmed that way. But I couldn't help thinking that protection can be a disguise for control, and romance, sometimes, is just a prettier word for possession.

So I watched him, again, like the anthropologist that I am. He was a pale, muscular relic of an emotional Ice Age, a world that still hasn't figured out what masculinity is supposed to mean now. He wasn't bad. He was lost.

We went out once more. This time, I questioned him deeply, pushing past the theatrics to get at the man. He wasn't ready for that conversation with me. It's okay. We were at my place, and I made the decision I rarely made then: I walked myself out of the situation without drama or waiting to be held back or guilted. I offered him a quiet exit out the back if he needed it.

Brazil and Argentina had tried. It wasn't a war this time, just a scrimmage. But we both knew—it wasn't the final.

Cultural Glimpse - The Argentinian

In Argentina, love is a rivalry—intense, lyrical, and always one goal away from drama. Men posture like matadors and charm like tango dancers. Victor didn't flirt, he challenged, and I mistook the duel for desire.

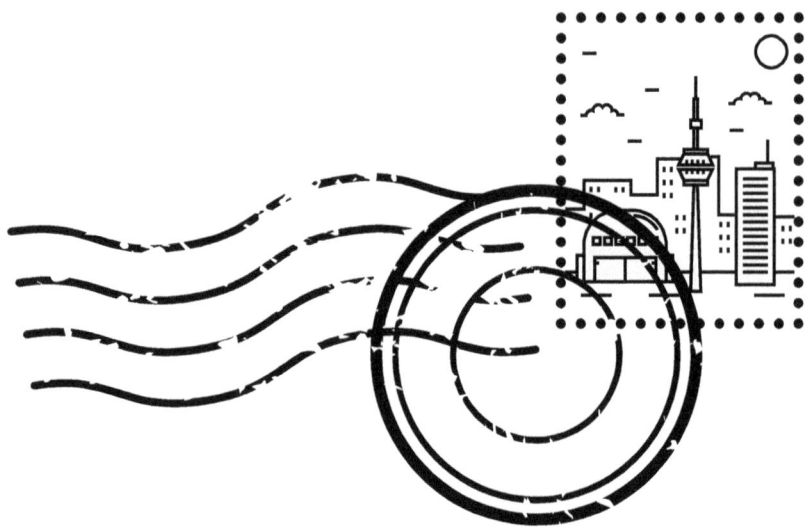

_____

_____

_____

_____

Date 35
Marco: The Italo-Canadian Firefighter

I wish I could say I made Marco up. That I conjured him out of a lonely Tuesday and a glass of red wine. But no. Marco was real. Real enough to set off the sprinklers.

Italian from Emilia-Romagna, he looked like he'd stepped out of a firefighter calendar someone's nonna kept under her bed. Medium tan skin, arms that belonged in an action film, and a jawline carved by espresso and miracles. I once was a firefighter myself. I never found them attractive — too familiar, too brotherly. But time softens edges, and Marco was no brother. He was the flame I hadn't realized I wanted to walk through.

We met on a dating app. Casual. Flirty. Ridiculous, really. But when we met, he smelled like eucalyptus and risk. And suddenly, I wasn't so immune. There wasn't a long love story. Just a spark. An awakening.

He reminded me that fantasy still had a place in my life. That sometimes a crush is sacred. That a man can be both a metaphor and a real human with good shoulders and decent intentions. Marco didn't stay. He didn't have to. He lit a match. And I remembered I was still fireproof.

35 - Marco:

I wish I could take credit for having created such a perfectly orchestrated man. That's how Marco felt—scripted by the gods of desire, wrapped in a uniform, and dropped into my life like a well-timed plot twist.

Marco was Italian, from Emilia-Romagna, though I only remember that thanks to the notes I took along the way. He had the skin tone of a late August evening, with summer still clinging to him. His was a medium build, but he was carved like someone who didn't need a gym because his body was the gym. He was the kind of man you'd expect to see on the cover of an Australian firefighter calendar, holding a puppy and melting housewives by the dozen.

He was also a real firefighter, which, ironically, should've made him immediately unattractive to me. After having been a firefighter myself, firefighters weren't men to me; they were brothers and comrades. To me, firefighters were people you trusted to carry your weight, not your fantasies.

But time passed, and life softened. And Marco reignited something I hadn't felt in years.

I tried to intellectualize it and turn my desire into data. Back in Brazil, we have something called Clube das Mulheres, or the Women's Club. Think of it as a strip club but feminine. It's sensual, not sexual. It's a place where women go not for nudity but for a story with men dressed as doctors, pilots, and firefighters acting out safe, seductive fantasies where women are the center. The gaze is ours. This doesn't involve submission, instruction, or obeying desire—it's more so about playing with desire and having a rehearsal space for feminine power. In Canada, though, fantasy is often treated with suspicion. Here, women are expected to be either effortlessly cool or hyper-liberated but never silly or craving. Fantasies involving uniforms or power dynamics get pathologized. You're seen as weak for wanting it, or worse, as being manipulated by the patriarchy.

But in Brazil, we know the difference, and we know play when we see it. So when Marco offered to do a private version of the Clube das Mulheres performance—as a joke, but not really—I said yes. And I meant it.

He stood there in my apartment, sirens echoing faintly from the city outside, giving me a private firefighter strip tease. He was fully clothed at first, but then pieces of clothing came off. It was never crude or mechanical. It was performance but with reverence.

I had never laughed and gasped so hard at the same time. Marco wore the role of "firefighter" differently than I ever had. For me, it had been sweat, duty, silence, and sacrifice. For him, it was also lightness, celebration, and play.

In that moment, I realized something important: women deserve sensual and primal fantasies, too.

We should be able to allow ourselves to freely engage in fantasies that involve authority, protection, and being wanted not for our potential or our personality but simply because we're there and desirable. Marco reminded me of that.

He wasn't trying to own me or fool me. He was just dancing the line between archetype and authenticity and doing it damn well.

We didn't date for long. I knew he was a bit of a player. Adrenaline was his currency, and he needed heat to feel alive. But that didn't make what we shared any less real.

He gave me something no previous firefighter ever had: permission to enjoy the fantasy, to let go of duty, to be silly, and to be a sensual woman.

When he left, it wasn't dramatic—just the gentle closing of a door behind a good fire. That was enough.

Cultural Glimpse – The Italian-Canadian

In Italian homes, boys grow up adored and taught to protect, pose, and please. Add a Canadian badge, and you get duty with a dimple. Marco was heat in uniform and fantasy with a pulse. He didn't need to seduce me—I arrived already burning.

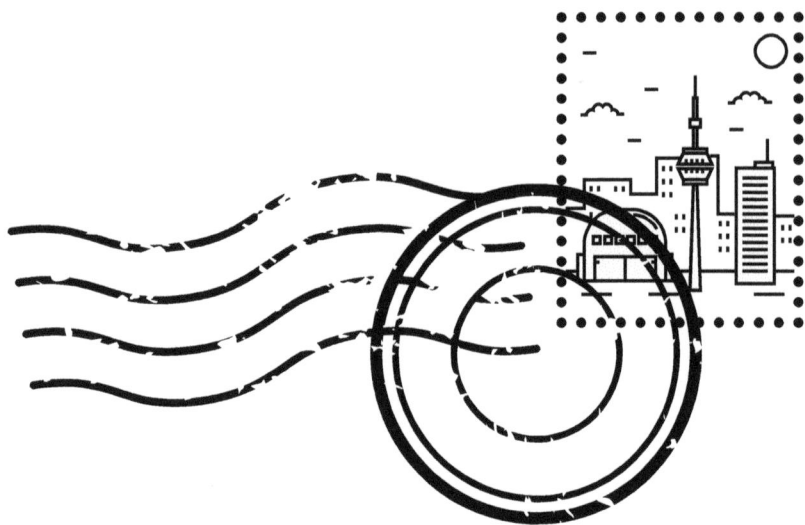

Date 36
Izidoro: The Italian
Things We Just Can't Help

We never met. Not really.
Izidoro was a friend-of-a-friend setup—my best friend, in fact, who had an impeccable record and a heart full of romantic optimism. She swore he was "exactly what I needed." Tall, charming, emotionally available. The works. And maybe he was. Until I saw the nose.

One nose. That's all it took. Not just any nose—his nose. The same exact nose as Adrian's. The heartbreak. The betrayal. The ghost I thought I'd already exorcised.

I froze.

Not metaphorically—literally. My nervous system went offline. My libido called in sick. My curiosity evaporated. I told my friend some vague excuse, but the truth was simple: I couldn't do it. It wasn't about Izidoro. He had done nothing wrong. He was just a man with the right nose at the wrong time. But trauma has a scent. And sometimes... a profile. And that's the thing about healing: it's not linear, and it's definitely not logical. You can date thirty-nine people and still get ambushed by a nostril. Izidoro may never know we were almost a story. But I do. And I've learned—some things you just can't override.

Especially when they smell like Adrian.

36 - Izidoro:

I enjoy dating. I love the stories, the spark, the newness, and the adventure of it all.

Maria, on the other hand, was exhausted by proxy by all the dating stories I've shared with her. She wanted me to take someone home already. Ideally, this person won't ghost, gaslight, or forget my birthday. "Enough adventures," she said while updating my location sharing. "I just want to track you on a date and not worry you're being emotionally waterboarded."

She wasn't joking. Maria is the kind of best friend who shares her calendar with me to keep my love life organized and shares my location with herself for safety, or control, or entertainment (it's probably all three).

She's the mother of my godson, the CEO of my emotional recovery team, and the unofficial head of my dating audit committee. She tracks my dates like NASA tracks spacecraft. If I don't text within two hours, she calls. If I don't respond, she sends memes. If the meme doesn't get a blue check, she assumes I've either fallen in love...or off a balcony.

One day, she made a declaration. "You need to meet this guy."

"No, Maria. I do not."

"Yes. You do. His name is Izidoro," she said, almost singing.

Izidoro? The name alone sounded like a red flag dipped in espresso.

She was beaming. "He just moved into our building. TTC driver. Great guy. Jorge likes him."

I raised a brow. "Jorge also thinks boiled eggs are a gourmet meal."

Maria waved it off. "He's solid. You'll like him. Just trust me."

I did not. But Maria had a way of cornering me with love and manipulation. I mean, wine was involved.

The plan was simple: I'd meet him at her place. It would be a chill night, low pressure, and no setup vibes.

Two days before the wine night, I stopped by to see my godson. I was walking into the building when he came out of the elevator, and time just stopped. He was tall, calm, confident, and kind-looking. He smiled and said, "Hello," with warmth and charm.

As he passed me, I saw it—His huge Italian nose, just like Adrian's. That kind of nose was my weakness and my curse. My brain went completely offline. I don't know what either of us said. I don't know if I said anything.

Maria watched the whole scene in slow motion. "She's got a headache," she announced like a telenovela actress showing up late to a dramatic scene, wrapping her arm around me told him, gently covering for my silent mental breakdown.

A headache? Girl, I needed a sedative.

I never showed up to the wine night. I didn't text or explain. Izidoro never knew what hit him.

It was the shortest date of my life: one minute in a hallway, zero glasses of wine, one devastating nose.

Fun fact: Later, Maria discovered that Izidoro actually had a super sexy girlfriend who was ten years older than him. Apparently, she was smart, stunning, and confident.

I fist-pumped the air. Go her! May all Italian noses be loved by bold women who know exactly what they want.

Cultural Glimpse - The Italian

In Italy, features are worn like family crests—noses, tempers, and charm passed down proudly. Romance is dramatic, almost operatic. But not every opera is worth the ticket. Izidoro wasn't the right nose for me—but my body didn't know that yet.

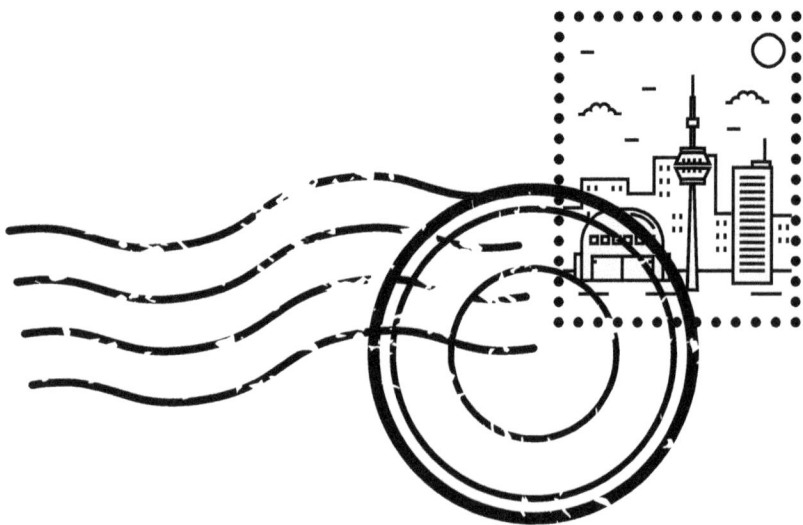

Date 37
Valentin: The Berlin Wall and the Bear

I was running from love like a spell that had gone sour. Until I hit a wall. A real one—German, Russian, and impossibly solid. His name was Valentin.

He looked like a prince carved from frost and iron. Ballroom dancer's poise, soldier's silence. The kind of man who didn't seduce you with words—but with presence. No games. No noise. Just warmth tucked inside discipline.

We met over candlelight and Cuban rum, under the city's soft chaos. I was testing fate; he was simply... there. With quiet eyes and a soft, almost reluctant smile. He made space without chasing. He steadied the room.

Valentin had a way of looking at you like you were already forgiven. Already chosen. He didn't come bearing armor or roses. He came with timing. With kindness. With truth. If I was the girl who lost her slipper at every ball, Valentin was the one who asked if I even wanted it back. He didn't awaken the storm. He offered shelter from it... and maybe, just maybe, that's what love becomes after all the dragons, after all the wars: Not the one who finds you at your best. But the one who stays... when you're still becoming.

37 - Valentin:

As I was running from my past, like the devil from the cross, as Catholics say, I stumbled into Valentin.

Catholicism had a twisted sense of humor. Just as I grew more spiritual, it gifted me a Valentine of its own. He was a man of contradictions and compassions, a German-Russian blend poured into a ballroom dancer's frame and military discipline.

He told me his name came from a novel. His Russian mother, regal like a leftover from the Romanov dynasty, had read a book about Spanish warriors. The hero's name was Valentin, and she vowed her son would be as brave.

I met him on an app—where else do modern miracles unfold? Match.com. What caught my eye was a photo of him mid-dance pose. He was German-Russian, raised between military bases, trained in precision and posture, and he danced.

I messaged him, intrigued. We agreed to meet at my "office": a Cuban restaurant I had come to treat like a second home. Naty, my Brazilian ally, also worked there. She would give the silent thumbs-up or wave the red flag mid-date. Some people have angels, but I had waitstaff.

Valentin had warned me—almost formally—that punctuality mattered to him. He was on German time. I laughed to myself. My people run on "Caribbean time," which mostly means juggling twelve things and forgetting one.

That day, I showed up early. I wore lipstick the color of protest. He walked in, tall and handsome, and spotted me. At our table, he told me about his life, his military schooling, and his German-Russian background. His parents' peoples were former enemies, and he'd grown up across Europe—Germany, Poland, Estonia—learning to live in transition. Then one day, he transitioned all the way to Canada to practice his English.

He passed all my five-star checks with ease. Education? Yes. Family-oriented? Deeply. No vices, no snoring (yet), and willing to consider a future with or without children. I was ready to draft up the paperwork.

But I still needed to be sure. For me, love had become like a PhD thesis. Passion was no longer enough—I needed fieldwork.

So, we agreed to meet again. Date two. He said he'd take me to the fairgrounds by the CN Tower. I liked the idea because it was playful, nostalgic, and dangerous in the right way.

What I didn't know was that I was walking into a training ground.

The fairgrounds shimmered with neon absurdity: stuffed animals, frying oil, and teenagers screaming on metal swings. Valentin walked beside me, tall, calm, and calculating. Then he walked up to a shooting game booth. Without a word, he just picked up the fake rifle like it was an extension of his arm. He squinted once, then—bang, bang, bang. Every target dropped.

I stood still, genuinely stunned.

He turned to me as if slightly concerned by my silence. "I'm sorry," he said. "It's... muscle memory."

"From what?" I asked, trying to make sense of it.

He sighed. "Military school. It's a thing in my family."

He handed me the prize—a giant teddy bear the size of my pride. I didn't know whether to laugh or salute. That's when I realized: the man could handle pressure, and he could do it with precision.

For our third meeting, it was my turn to impress. I took him to a Brazil vs. France Olympic soccer game. The real test.

I screamed, cursed, and jumped up and down, becoming the human version of a Brazilian flag with vocal cords. He didn't flinch once, not even when I gave the ref the finger. He just smiled and handed me water like I was a dehydrated athlete.

That's when I knew he was anchored. Valentin didn't try to change me or flinch away from me. We weren't in love yet. But we liked each other a lot, trying each other on like warm coats, seeing what fit.

I learned something profound from him. Strength doesn't always roar, but sometimes, it simply holds space.

We were the walking proof that trauma can skip a generation and become kindness. That night, when I walked home with a giant bear in my arms and the smell of sugar in my hair, I thought, If peace had a posture, it might look like him.

Cultural Glimpse – The German-Russian

In Berlin, emotion walks in boots that are measured, direct, and weatherproof. From Russia, he carried discipline. From Germany, structure. But his heart was as soft as snowfall. Valentin didn't break walls; he waited by them. Slowly, I opened the gate.

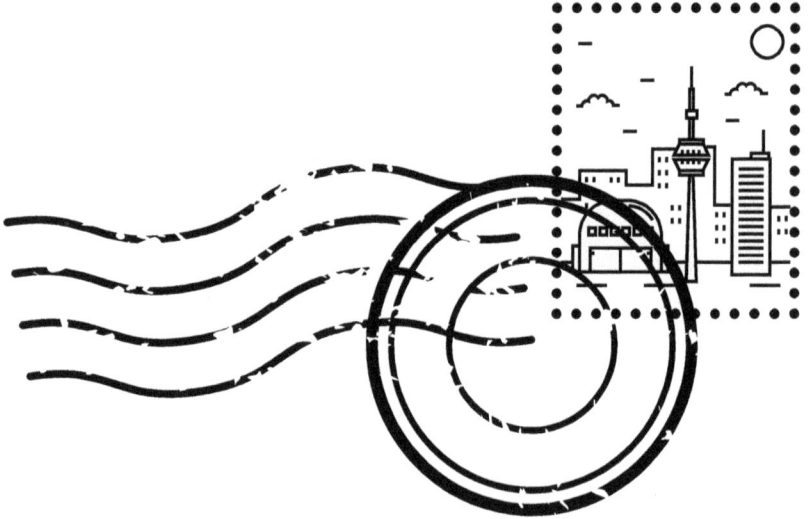

Date 38
Phillip: A Polish Illusion of a Dream

There are men who make you question your standards. And then there are men who meet every single one—yet still, something inside you says no. Not yet.

Phillip was the kind of man women say they want. Steady. Kind. Emotionally available. He knew who he was and what he wanted—and he wanted me. Not in the possessive way that some men want you, like a trophy or a missing piece. He wanted me in a quiet, intentional way. The kind that says: I've done the work. I'm ready.

He was what I used to think love should look like. If love were a checklist, Phillip would have passed with flying colors. But here's the thing about checklists: they don't measure soul. With Phillip, I wasn't trying to decode texts. I wasn't over-analyzing his tone or wondering if he was lying. I wasn't bracing for disappointment. And in that safety, I found my own clarity.

This is not a story of heartbreak. It's a story of deep gratitude. It's the story of learning that sometimes, you don't walk away from someone because they're not good enough. You walk away because you finally are.

38 - Phillip:

The first time I saw Phillip, I could already imagine our life together. It's not that he was perfect, but there was something so unmistakably right about him that it was hard not to picture a future. I met him on eHarmony, and yes, it was one of those sites that asked you fifty million questions about yourself, almost as if the universe itself were trying to size you up. For me, $165 a year seemed like a small price to pay for a chance at the perfect match. Phillip was one of those matches that made you raise an eyebrow in disbelief, like, "Is this real?"

I couldn't help but smile when I saw his picture. He was tall, fair--skinned, and had a baby face that seemed to belong on a Pampers box. I couldn't decide whether I wanted to pinch his cheeks or just keep him in my pocket for safekeeping. He was that kind of adorable, the type of man you see on family holiday cards, the one you always secretly hoped you'd end up with.

Phillip was the kind of guy who wore his heart out in the open. There was nothing about him that was complicated or ambiguous. He made it clear from the start that he wanted a family and that he wanted me to be part of that family. It was both flattering and terrifying. I think we all dream about finding someone who wants to build a future with us, but I wasn't sure I was ready to do that with him—at least not in the way he imagined it.

One of the first things he did that made me smile was how easy it was to be with him. We went on dates where the conversations flowed effortlessly, where it felt as though we'd known each other for years. It was a quiet kind of comfort, like a favorite sweater you never want to take off.

The first time we spent an entire weekend together was a trip to Wasaga Beach. The simplicity of this getaway was so beautiful, it almost seemed like a dream. Phillip was fun and sweet—an easy-going guy who was great with the little things. He'd help me with my bag, open doors, and do all the things that made me feel cared for. But it wasn't just that. He made me feel seen. I never had to explain anything twice. He was present in a way that felt both safe and comforting.

But even then, there was a quiet tension hanging in the background. Phillip was so open, so ready to build something with me, that I felt the weight of it pressing against me. I wasn't ready. Not yet. I didn't want to be the person who held him back and couldn't give him what he wanted. He made me feel as if I were the one, but in the deepest part of me, I knew my heart wasn't all the way there.

On my birthday, things came to a head. Valentin had always been there, lingering in my heart and in my thoughts, even though I never fully acknowledged it to Phillip. The night we celebrated my birthday, I invited both Valentin and Phillip. This wasn't just a birthday dinner-

—I was sitting at the intersection of two versions of my life. There were moments during the evening when I caught myself wondering if I was doing the right thing or if I was the one for either of them. But I knew, deep down, I wasn't ready to let go of Valentin yet.

Phillip and I continued seeing each other, but I couldn't pretend anymore. We were moving in different directions, and no amount of sweet gestures, cozy weekend trips, or innocent baby-face smiles could change that. I could feel my feelings for Valentin growing, expanding in a way that was undeniable. Phillip, on the other hand, wanted more, and it felt like too much pressure, too soon.

It wasn't that Phillip wasn't perfect. He was everything I had once imagined as "the one." But sometimes, even when things seem perfect on paper, the heart doesn't always follow. And my heart had already chosen.

Phillip took it better than I had expected. We talked about it, and I explained where I was. We both knew where this was headed, and I could tell it was hard for him. But he said something that stayed with me: "I will allow him to be your next boyfriend because I'll be your last. I will wait."

Those words, spoken with such sincerity, hit me in a way I couldn't shake. What do you do with that? What do you do when someone is willing to wait for you, even when you know you can't give them what they want? How do you walk away from someone who is so kind, so honest, and so unflinchingly committed?

Phillip and I let go of each other, but the memory of that vow stayed with me long after. I don't know if I'll ever fully understand how or why he could love me so openly, so freely, but I do know that he is a man who believes in love, in family, and in waiting for the right person—even if that person can't always give him what he deserves.

Phillip wasn't "the one" for me, but he was the right one for someone else. Maybe he will always be my "what if," but I can't help but think he would have been the one for a different version of me.

Cultural Glimpse - The Canadian Ideal

In Canada, stability is the fairytale—clean, kind, and quietly committed. Phillip was everything I was told to want: open-hearted, ready, good. But sometimes, what you're supposed to want isn't what you need.

Date 39
Michael: The Israeli Paradox

ichael introduced himself as Mike, but it didn't fit. He was a full-syllable man—layered, articulate, emotionally complex. Our first date lasted ten hours. We talked about everything: divorce, kids, cooking, politics, grief. He was the kind of man I could talk to forever. The kind that made you feel chosen by his curiosity. But then we had our second date—in public.

That's when Mike showed up. A man who sent food back with disdain, corrected waiters with ego, and seemed allergic to kindness if anyone else was watching. It wasn't standards—it was performance. Inside, he was Michael. Outside, he became someone else entirely.

I gave him one last date—half in public, half private. One final test. And again, he failed. At the end, he began describing "our future," including my "new boobs," as if he were assembling a better girlfriend on a factory line. I smiled and said, "I've made my choice.

I'm choosing Valentin."

He paused. Then:

"Of course. You picked the German."

That's when I knew.

Michael was real, but only behind closed doors.

And I? I was done dating men who could only be kind in secret.

39 - Michael:

My last date before everything changed was with an Israeli man named Michael. He was a chef and a builder, the kind of man who could talk for hours and build you a kitchen from scratch. The first time we met, I called him Michael, not Mike, which is how he introduced himself. Mike didn't fit. I didn't think about it much at the time—it was instinctive. Nicknames have always been my thing. Michael, as a name, felt sacred, like something his mother had whispered into his curls as a child. I found out later that she was the only other person who called him that, but she had passed.

We met through the eHarmony site, which makes you answer fifty questions just to prove you're serious. At the time, I was trying to be serious. Michael was my match, according to their charts and formulas. Maybe the algorithm knew something I didn't, or maybe it was just cruel.

Our first date lasted ten hours. We talked about everything—his divorce, his kids, food, pain, hope, cities we'd loved, and people we'd lost. I remember thinking: this is someone I could talk to for a lifetime. He was a rare build-in best friend type. He made me laugh and made me think. His eyes were bright and wild and knowing. That night, we walked to my place, sat on the couch, and kept going, no touching, just talk.

I liked Michael. Alone, he was remarkable. He could teach a seminar on charm and intimacy, and the curriculum would make you believe.

But then, there was the second date. In the outside world, Michael was someone else entirely. We had a whole day planned, but the moment we stepped into public space, he transformed. He barked at waiters, sending back meat like he had been personally betrayed. He criticized everything: the cut of the meat, the texture, and the plating. Everything was a battle. He walked through the world like it owed him an apology.

Sitting across from him at lunch, I listened as his voice deepened into an unrecognizable baritone. It was a tone you use when claiming territory.

I started to feel small, like prey in a dry savanna. He made life outside feel dangerous. Inside, he was Michael. Outside, he was Mike—armored, relentless, rehearsed. It was shocking how easily he switched.

It was then I realized that I didn't want to go through life in hiding with someone. I didn't want to dim myself just to survive lunch. Still, I gave him a third date out of respect for our mutual honesty. He knew I was seeing others, and I had told him if I found clarity, I'd say so.

We planned a half-day out, half-day in. This was the final exam. The first half was more of the same. He criticized everything again—this time with flair. There was the wrong napkin texture and the "mediocre" lighting. It was like he wanted me to snap at him. But I didn't. Instead, I smiled with composure. My performance was Oscar-worthy. It was like he didn't know what to do with that. He watched me closely, studying like maybe he'd misjudged me or the scene.

By the time we were alone again, he leaned back, victorious. "Now that we're on the same page," he said, "we can start planning our life together." And then he told me what that life would look like. This included, of course, the new boobs I would be getting. He said he felt that would be "more appropriate," like he was giving me a kitchen upgrade. I found this funny because I had done a breast reduction recently, and I liked my breasts just fine. They were staying the way they were.

I had to speak up for myself. "Mike," I said softly.

His eyes flashed because it was the first time I ever called him that. "I'm choosing Valentin."

He just nodded slowly, like the final move in a chess game had been made.

I had something else waiting for me. A different kind of love and a different kind of truth. I was finally ready.

Cultural Glimpse - The Israeli

In Israel, love is urgent, born of contrast, carved by conflict, pulsing with possibility. Men grow up fast there, taught to lead, to fight, to survive with charm. Michael wore two faces: one for the crowd and one for the quiet. I fell for the man behind the performance, but he lived on stage.

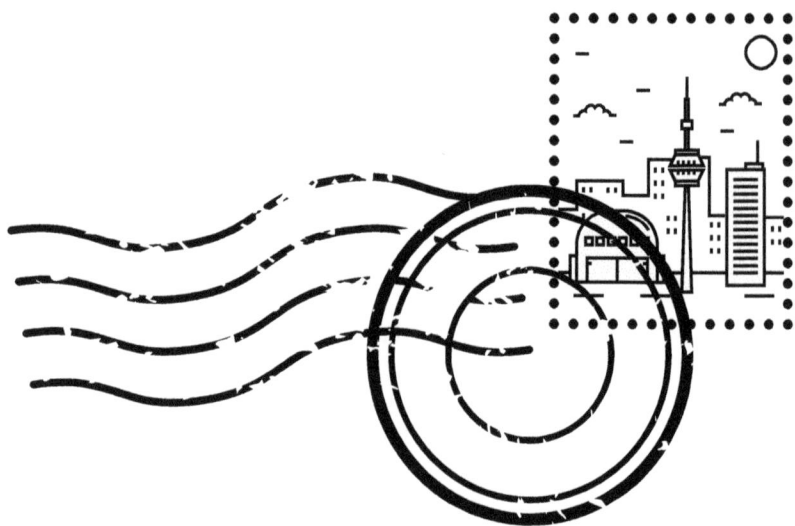

Chapter 40
Simone: Th3 Black Cat

Some stories don't end. They loop. They return when you're no longer looking, wearing a new dress, a darker perfume, a clearer truth. Simone came back like that.

Not as a lover, not even as a woman—but as a symbol. A riddle. A mirror I had buried under 38 lessons and one unanswered question: Why not me?

By then, I had dated an army. Loved, lost, and laughed at myself in enough languages to earn a minor in anthropology. I'd built a map of men, one heartbreak at a time. But Simone? Simone was the legend in the margins. The myth I'd bookmarked, hoping the ending would change.

Toronto felt quieter that week. Maybe it was just me. I was quieter too.

There are women we meet who awaken desire. Others who awaken memory. And then there are the ones who awaken choice. Simone was that. Not a storm, not a savior. A spell.

This wasn't about romance. It never was. This was about returning to the scene of the becoming—not to ask, but to know. Not to take back the power, but to bless it. To ask the devil a question and thank him for the fire. Because sometimes, the final chapter isn't about closure.

It's about walking into the ritual with your own matches.

Wearing lace.

Carrying wine. And speaking the name of the woman you finally became—Th3 Black Cat.

40 - Th3 Black Cat:

Something still gnawed at me. I had dated, danced, meditated, healed. I had kissed strangers and forgiven ghosts. And still... I was missing a piece.

It wasn't love I was after. It was truth. Not just any truth—his truth. I had never asked Alex the real question, the one that could unlock the riddle of my own becoming: Why did you choose Simone?

If I was ever going to understand the kind of partnership I deserved—one where I was picked not out of need, but of want—then I needed to hear it from the man himself.

I saw the green dot beside his name and I messaged him.

As if no time had passed, he responded with smooth, theatrical charm:

"Ah... a bliss from the past. Always nice to see you."

"Alex, I have a question," I replied. "Something I need to understand."

He paused, then answered with a flicker of the mischief that used to keep me tangled.

"Don't we all, gatinha preta?"

Then came his offer. "I'll tell you anything you want. No filters, no edits. But..."

"But?"

"I want to watch."

"Watch what?"

"You and Simone. Talking. Drinking. Laughing. Undressing each other. Maybe more. I don't need to be involved. I just want to witness it. Like an artist watching his favorite painting. Like a sinner remembering grace. Like someone who knows exactly what he gave up."

There was a long stretch of quiet before he continued.

"You want your answer. I want my vision."

What he proposed didn't feel like surrender, and it didn't feel like a trap. It felt like a transaction written in desire and sealed with nerve. I called it Sacrieasy, a word that shouldn't have made sense, and yet it did—both sacrament and indulgence, sacred and effortless.

I said yes.

Not out of rebellion, not to provoke him or prove something, but because I was finally ready to understand myself without apology or disguise.

I took my time getting ready, choosing everything with intention. No jeans, no beige, no borrowed softness. I wasn't arriving as the good girl or the careful ex. I was Th3 Black Cat. I wasn't performing the role of the healer or the one who always stays kind.

I was stepping into something else entirely.

I lined my lips in a deep, wine-stained red and slipped into a silk robe that moved like water. Beneath it, I wore black lace—not to impress anyone, not to seduce, but because it felt like my truth. The heels were sharp enough to be taken seriously. The perfume behind each ear was quiet and certain, like a secret I wasn't trying to keep.

When I looked in the mirror, I saw the woman I would choose if I had the chance to fall in love for the first time again. I was finally willing to choose myself.

He had prepared everything with care. The candles flickered as if they knew more than they let on. The wine had already been poured. Simone sat beside him, poised and luminous, a quiet glint of curiosity in her eyes. It was as if part of her had also been waiting.

In the background, Brazilian MPB played. We lifted our glasses without a word. Then I turned to him and asked, "Alex, tell me. Why her?"

He didn't hesitate or deflect. He looked at me, then at Simone, and for once, there was no performance in his face.

"First," he said, voice steady and clear, "I miss her. Constantly. No matter where I am, I want to be near her. She brings peace to my head. She's the first person I want to talk to about everything—what's good, what's bad, what doesn't matter. Life feels better when she's next to me."

The words settled between us. Simone didn't turn away.

He went on. "Second—independência financeira."

I tilted my head. "Really?"

He nodded. "It's not just the money. It's how she carries herself through the world. She's with me because she chooses to be, not because she has to be. She walks beside me, never behind. She leans on me only when it's intentional. That kind of independence—it changes how a man sees everything."

He paused because he meant every word.

"If we had to go our separate ways tomorrow, I know she'd be fine. And I'd be fine. That's the trust between us. That's the strength. Knowing we're whole on our own, and still, every day, she wakes up and chooses me. That makes me feel like I matter."

It wasn't a list of qualities. It was a kind of alchemy—desire mixed with steadiness and respect folded into attraction. It was a balance between what's felt and what's earned.

I'm glad I spent a few hours with Alex and Simone because it confirmed something I was coming to terms with. I was finally ready to be fully myself—without edits, without apology. I was done being almost loved.

After thirty-nine dates, broken hopes, and detours disguised as lessons, I hadn't just arrived at another strange night.

I had stepped into a turning point.

This was a chapter in my own mythology.

And it marked the beginning of a new kind of magic.

Naquela noite, meu corpo era um feitiço. Meu desejo, a escolha.

That night, my body was a spell, my desire, the choice.

Cultural Glimpse - Th3 Black Cat

This one isn't about a country but the woman who walks through them all. She purrs through memory, prowls through myth, and waits at the edge of your becoming. This chapter wasn't a story. It's a spell. And it's already working.

The 40° LOVE – Becoming

I used to believe a love story needed a cinematic ending—a ring, an airport kiss, or a speech in the rain. I thought it had to be dramatic or polished. But I've learned that the true turning points are quieter. They settle into you. They arrive when you realize you've stopped waiting.

I didn't stumble into this chapter. I walked here—sometimes in heels, sometimes in sneakers, sometimes barefoot—through seasons of longing, heartbreak, and growth. I dated with intention. I looked for patterns, listened for meaning, and trusted the silence when it spoke louder than the words.

This is where I landed. I have no disguise and no role to perform. It's just me...and then, him. I call him Mr. Perfect.

Mr. Perfect doesn't lack flaws, but I no longer expect love to complete something it didn't break. I chose him only after I learned to stand with myself.

When I began writing, I thought I was collecting stories: little scenes from dates, cultural comparisons, sharp-edged observations wrapped in flirtation and humor. But something shifted halfway through, around Chapter 24. Simone. Also like, de Beauvoir.

Her name was Simone, and she didn't appear by chance. She was the turning point, the mirror, the place where the old narrative cracked. She didn't ask who I loved but how I loved.

Through her, I remembered something essential—that my freedom had never depended on the absence of men. It came from being fully present in my own life. Simone didn't rescue me, but she reminded me that I'd already begun to rise.

After that, the dates changed. The ache behind them faded. I was no longer searching for someone to prove something. I had started collecting truths, not trophies.

That's how I met him. There was no grand entrance. No lightning bolt. He showed up like a well-fit puzzle piece—quiet, certain, familiar.

It was an ordinary day, one I almost skipped. I'd grown tired of dating apps and tired of performing charm during forced conversations. But I showed up. Curiosity got me out the door.

The first thing I noticed was his eyes—kind, steady. He didn't rush his words. He had a way of listening that felt both easy and complete. We talked about garlic, music, and the absurd challenge of finding pants that fit. We laughed, paused, and let the space breathe.

When I walked away, I didn't think he was the one. I just felt calm. And that calm stayed with me.

Over time, I realized that feeling had a name: peace. It became the new standard for connection.

Loving him didn't feel like falling. It felt like waking up. I could wake up to the sound of my own laughter in a space that welcomed it. Soon, I was waking up beside someone who didn't question my worth, waking up in a relationship built not on fantasy but on rhythm, care, and mutual intention.

He was steady and quick to laugh. He listened without trying to fix. He didn't want me smaller. He wanted to know what kind of life I imagined, and he waited for the answer.

I told him about the book and the 39 dates. He didn't flinch or look uncomfortable.

He said, "You've lived."

I said, "I've learned."

"Tell me about it," he replied with a warm smile.

So I did over time between shared meals, quiet mornings, and the pauses where memory slips in unannounced. He never measured himself against my past. He understood that he belonged to my future.

The early chapters of this book followed a trail of questions. The later ones revealed the answers I'd been carrying all along.

I began to see more clearly—where I had limited myself, where I had absorbed stories that didn't belong to me, and who I had become through it all.

I came to understand that being "too much" was another way of being powerful. That dignity and desire could live side by side. That curiosity had always been an act of courage.

And that love—sustaining, grounded love—grows not in sparks but in soil.

We didn't burst into being. We grew. We didn't rush. We took root.

This book isn't an instruction manual for finding a partner. It's a record of choosing myself again and again.

He didn't complete me; he confirmed me. This was proof that I had done the work and had become a woman who no longer waits to be chosen. I had already chosen to speak, to walk away, to stay with discomfort, to feel, and to tell the truth, even when it unsettled the room. That was the turning point. Not meeting him. Becoming myself.

So, let me pause here and speak directly to you. Thank you for coming this far. Thank you for reading through 39 dates, each its own little world. Thank you for staying with me in the moments that made you laugh or made you ache. Thank you for meeting this story on its own terms.

This isn't a fairy tale. This is fieldwork.

And love—real love—grows in the field. In the dirt. In the tending. In the days when nothing blooms and the ones when everything does.

It asks for presence, attention, and fluency in a language that doesn't always rely on words.

Love, I've come to see, doesn't involve being saved. Love is knowing you are already free.

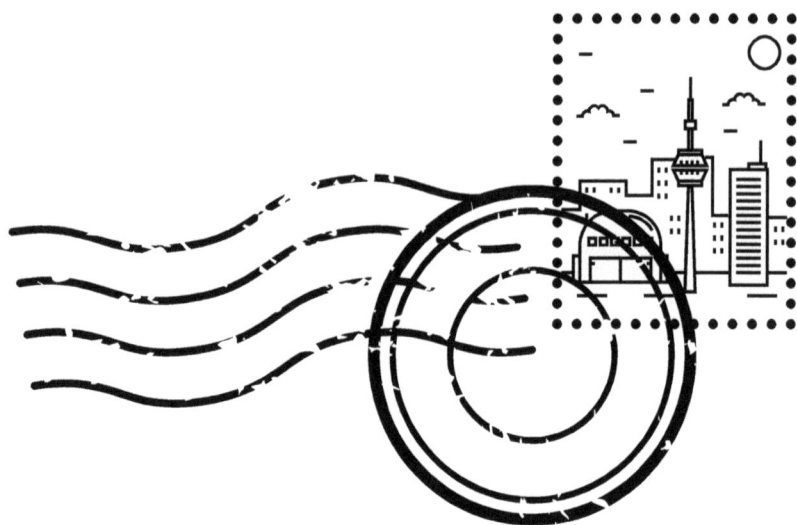

Epilogue
Meow...

They say if you date enough people, you'll find the one. That was never the point for me. I wasn't searching for a finish line; I was finding myself.

The 39 men weren't mistakes but mirrors, prisms, and gateways. Each one carried a clue, a question, a challenge, or a gift—sometimes all four.

Some men cracked me open. Others stitched me back together in places I didn't know were torn. A few men were hurricanes. Others, soft rains. But every one of them brought me closer to my truest self.

I once thought the quest was to understand more about romantic love that people write sonnets about or fight wars for. But in the end, it was something quieter, wilder, more honest than that.

I learned to see myself through the clarity of my own curiosity without caring about the opinion of those who adored me or abandoned me.

I chose me, and I wasn't a consolation prize but the main character in a story I'm still writing. This is a coming-of-age tale wrapped in the shiny bow of modern dating. This "fairytale" ending isn't an ending at all; it's the beginning of me breaking the spell of other people's expectations and turning wounds into wisdom.

In the end, there was no prince; just a woman, present in her power, wearing black lace, and speaking the truth.

I finally found what I was looking for after all. Me.

Psst...

If you made it this far, maybe you're not just a reader.
Maybe you're a teacher.
A guide.
A rebel with questions too big for one language.
A woman who knows that love is political —and personal —and
worth studying with the same reverence we give to books on law, bio-
logy, or war.
Turn to the end of this book.
There's a guide waiting for you — written in three tongues, for all
the women you've been.
It doesn't have answers.
But it might unlock some of yours.

(see: Discussion Guide – Gender, Power, and the Politics of Love)

Note on Discussion Guide

I created this guide in three languages, using the same examples in each. It wasn't just a matter of translation – it was an act of weaving bridges. I wanted women who read this book, wherever they are, to find themselves in the same stories, to speak about the same wounds, to laugh at the same metaphors. I wanted them to begin conversations that transcend borders, accents, and the illusions that keep us apart. Because if love has taught me anything, it is that our questions are often the same – only our words differ.

Discussion Guide

Included in all copies of LOVE [DATED]
(English • Português • Español)

Foreword / Prefácio / Prólogo

This is not a manual.

This is a mirror.

This guide was not designed to teach what love is, but to help us unlearn the stories we were told — about who gets to feel safe, who gets to speak, who is worthy of softness, and who carries the burden of always knowing what to do.

Let this be a space where your answers don't have to be final. Let this be a place where your questions are free to evolve.

You are allowed to change your mind here. You are allowed to be many.

Are you ready? To question love, gender, power, and the lies we inherited? Are you ready to meet the woman you are when you stop performing the woman they expect?

Welcome to the practice of coexistability — the sacred, plural act of being more than one thing at once.

Educator's Discussion Guide: Gender, Power, and the Politics of Love

Based on LOVE [DATED] by Nia Yara

Purpose of the Guide

This guide supports educators in using LOVE [DATED] as a tool to explore gender equality, emotional intelligence, and cultural identity through the lens of real-life, multicultural love stories. Each chapter becomes a gateway into deeper societal analysis, while preserving the emotional truths and intimate questions that resonate with students across diverse backgrounds.

Learning Outcomes

After engaging with this book, students should be able to:

1.   Reflect critically on how gender roles and expectations manifest in romantic and cultural contexts.

2.   Identify and challenge patriarchal dynamics in relationships and society.

3.   Examine how culture, race, migration, and class intersect with intimacy and gender expression.

4.   Develop emotional literacy by analyzing personal narratives and the politics of desire.

5.   Engage in respectful, intersectional dialogue around complex issues of identity and power.

Discussion Modules (Optional or Sequential)

Each module corresponds with themes present in the book and offers prompts, activities, and reflection tools.

Module 1: The Body, The Field, The First Exit
(Based on the Introduction & Chapter 0)

Themes: Safety, Consent, Sovereignty, Women's Intuition, Gendered Socialization

Discussion Questions:

• What does emotional or physical safety mean in the context of dating?

• Why is it necessary to speak of "safety protocols" before speaking of love?

• How do women internalize caution? How do men perceive it?

• What are the invisible labors of femininity in public and private life?

Activity:
Have students write a short reflective letter to their younger self or future self on what "boundaries" mean to them today.

Module 2: The Mask of Charm

(Choose chapters like Stephan – The Nigerian Charmer or Savvas – The Cultural Trap)

Themes: Performance, Toxic Romance, Gendered Seduction, Emotional Intelligence

Discussion Questions:

• How is charm used as a social tool? When does it become manipulation?

• How does gender influence who performs and who is expected to be "authentic"?

• Can emotional sensitivity be a form of control?

Class Exercise:

Role-play a date scene and pause to identify microdynamics: who is leading the interaction, what power is unspoken, what scripts are at play?

Module 3: Cultural Desire and the Exotification Trap

(Chapters like Ali – The Afghan-German Drift, or Simone – The French)

Themes: Race, Exoticization, Queer Desire, Diaspora, Double Standards

Discussion Questions:

• What does it mean to be desired "as a type"? How does that feel?

• How are gender and race entangled in the way we choose partners?

• What is the difference between curiosity and objectification?

Activity:
Students analyze one pop culture relationship (TV, film, celebrity) through a gender + race lens. Who gets to be idealized? Who gets objectified?

Module 4: The Invisible Test – Masculinity and Emotional Labor
(Chapters like Ewan – The Riddle Man or Phillip – The Snowball Dream)

Themes: Masculinity, Communication Gaps, Emotional Compatibility, Feminine Work
Discussion Questions:

• What emotional labor is often assumed to be "women's work"?

• What does a "test" in relationships look like—and is it fair?

• How are men socialized to deal with love, rejection, or intimacy?

Reflection:
Write about one moment in your life when you had to translate your needs. Was your counterpart listening?

Module 5: Freedom, Faith, and the Feminine
(Chapters like Sri – The Uniform of Grace or Simone – The French)

Themes: Feminine Power, Spirituality, Ethics in Love, Autonomy

Discussion Questions:

• What does it mean to choose rather than to fall in love?

• Can you be both emotionally free and deeply connected?

• How do cultural and spiritual beliefs shape your view of commitment?

Creative Task:
Design a "contract of love" with clauses that reflect your own values—freedom, support, growth, desire, etc.

Assessment Suggestions (for classrooms)

• Journaling Portfolio – personal reflections on 3 chapters

• Comparative Essay – contrast one story from the book with a cultural or literary example

• Group Project – Present a modern "dating ethnography" using interviews and analysis

• Critical Book Review – focused on gender equality, using evidence from the text

Key Teaching Reminders

• Encourage self-reflection, not confession. Keep discussions emotionally safe.

• Reinforce the idea that gender equality includes men's emotional healing.

• Highlight that multicultural relationships bring insight, but also layers of complexity.

PORTUGUÊS

Este não é um manual.
É um espelho.
Este guia não foi feito para ensinar o que é o amor, mas para nos aju-
dar a desaprender as histórias que nos contaram — sobre quem merece
segurança, quem tem o direito de falar, quem pode ser delicado, e quem
carrega o peso de saber sempre o que fazer.
Este é um espaço onde suas perguntas podem mudar.
Onde suas certezas não precisam durar. Você pode mudar de ideia
aqui. Você pode ser muitas.
Você está pronta? Para questionar o amor, o gênero, o poder e as
mentiras que herdamos?
Você está pronta para encontrar a mulher que você é quando para de
interpretar a mulher que esperam?
Bem-vinda à prática da coexistabilidade —o ato sagrado e plural de
coexistir com tudo o que você já foi e ainda é.

Guia de Discussão para Educadores: Gênero, Poder e a Política do Amor

Baseado no livro de Nia Yara – LOVE [DATED]

Objetivo do Guia

Este guia apoia educadores(as) no uso do livro LOVE [DATED] como ferramenta pedagógica para explorar temas como igualdade de gênero, afetividade consciente, interculturalidade e inteligência emocional a partir de histórias reais de amor vividas entre diferentes culturas. Cada capítulo oferece um ponto de partida para discussões profundas sobre identidade, poder e desejo, com linguagem acessível e uma abordagem crítica e sensível.

Competências Desenvolvidas

Ao final dos módulos, espera-se que estudantes:

- Reflitam criticamente sobre os papéis de gênero e como eles se manifestam nos relacionamentos.

- Compreendam as dinâmicas de poder entre homens e mulheres em diferentes contextos culturais.

- Desenvolvam a escuta empática e o pensamento crítico sobre o amor, o corpo e a autonomia.

• Analisem o impacto do racismo, do machismo e do colonialismo nas relações afetivas.

• Dialoguem de forma respeitosa e interseccional sobre temas sensíveis ligados à identidade e à intimidade.

Módulos de Discussão

Cada módulo traz temas centrais, perguntas provocativas, e sugestões de atividades pedagógicas.

Módulo 1: O Corpo, o Campo e a Primeira Saída
(Baseado na Introdução e Capítulo 0)

Temas: Segurança, Consentimento, Soberania Emocional, Intuição Feminina

Perguntas para debate:

• O que significa estar segura em um encontro?

• Por que é necessário falar sobre segurança antes de falar sobre amor?

• Como o medo molda a forma como mulheres amam?

• O que homens precisam ouvir sobre o que não sabem sobre a nossa vivência?

Atividade Sugerida:

Escreva uma carta ao seu "eu do passado" com conselhos sobre autocuidado e limites.

Módulo 2: A Máscara do Charme
(Capítulos como Stephan – O Galanteador Nigeriano ou Savvas – A Armadilha da Sensibilidade Cultural)

Temas: Performance Masculina, Sedução Tóxica, Inteligência Emocional

Perguntas para debate:

- Qual a diferença entre charme e manipulação?

- Como homens e mulheres performam afeto?

- Existe um "teatro" do amor? Quem ganha com ele?

Exercício em grupo:

Encenar um diálogo de conquista e, em grupo, pausar para analisar os códigos ocultos de poder e gênero.

Módulo 3: Desejo Cultural e o Perigo da Exotização
(Capítulos como Ali – O Afgão-Alemão ou Simone – A Francesa)

Temas: Raça, Desejo, Identidade, Queer, Feminilidade Livre

Perguntas para debate:

- Você já foi desejado(a) como um "tipo"? Como isso te fez sentir?

- Como o racismo pode atravessar até o amor?

- Qual a diferença entre admiração cultural e fetichização?

Atividade Crítica:

Escolher um casal de novela ou reality show e analisar as camadas raciais e de gênero que atravessam a relação.

Módulo 4: Os Testes Invisíveis – Masculinidades e Trabalho Emocional
(Capítulos como Ewan – O Escocês Enigmático ou Phillip – O Sonho de Neve)

Temas: Masculinidade, Comunicação, Afeto, Expectativas Emocionais
Perguntas para debate:

• Quais tarefas afetivas ainda recaem majoritariamente sobre as mulheres?

• O que são "testes invisíveis" nos relacionamentos e por que eles acontecem?

• Como as masculinidades podem ser mais conscientes e generosas?

Reflexão Escrita:

Relate um momento em que você não foi compreendido(a) emocionalmente. O que faltou?

Módulo 5: Liberdade, Fé e o Feminino
(Capítulos como Sri – O Policial Sikh ou Simone – A Francesa)

Temas: Espiritualidade, Autonomia, Desejo Ético, Escolhas

Perguntas para debate:

• O que significa escolher alguém conscientemente, e não "cair de amores"?

• Liberdade e compromisso podem coexistir?

• Como espiritualidade pode influenciar nossa forma de amar?

Criação Livre:

Escreva seu próprio "contrato de amor": o que é indispensável para você num relacionamento? (valores, limites, sonhos)

Sugestões de Avaliação

• Diário reflexivo: Entradas semanais com pensamentos e aprendizados pessoais.

• Ensaio crítico: Análise comparativa entre um capítulo do livro e uma obra cultural brasileira.

• Projeto de grupo: Criar um "mapa afetivo" da cidade com histórias anônimas de amor e machismo.

• Resenha feminista: Escrita com base em um dos capítulos e discussões em aula.

Leituras Complementares (opcional)

• Sejamos Todos Feministas – Chimamanda Ngozi Adichie

• O Segundo Sexo – Simone de Beauvoir

• A Vida Não É Útil – Ailton Krenak

- Mulheres, Raça e Classe – Angela Davis

- Tudo Nela Brilha e Queima – Ryane Leão

Dicas para o/a Educador(a)

- Evite exposição emocional forçada. Respeite os limites dos estudantes.

- Crie espaços seguros de escuta ativa.

- Traga exemplos reais e acessíveis do cotidiano escolar.

- Incentive os estudantes a aplicarem os conceitos na sua realidade afetiva e familiar.

ESPAÑOL

Esto no es un manual.

Es un espejo.

Esta guía no fue creada para definir qué es el amor, sino para ayudarnos a desaprender las historias heredadas —sobre quién merece estar segura, quién tiene voz,quién puede ser suave, y quién carga con la obligación de saber siempre qué hacer.

Este es un lugar donde tus preguntas pueden transformarse.

Donde tus respuestas no tienen que ser definitivas.

Aquí puedes cambiar de opinión. Aquí puedes ser muchas.

¿Estás lista?

Para cuestionar el amor, el género, el poder y las mentiras que nos enseñaron?

¿Estás lista para conocer a la mujer que eres cuando dejas de actuar como la mujer que esperan?

Bienvenida a la práctica de la coexistabilidad — el arte sagrado y múltiple de coexistir contigo misma, en todas tus formas.

Guía de Discusión para Educadores: Género, Poder y la Política del Amor

Basada en el libro de Nia Yara – LOVE [DATED]

Objetivo de la Guía

Esta guía fue creada para acompañar a docentes, facilitadores y educadores/as sociales en el uso del libro LOVE [DATED] como una herramienta pedagógica que invita a reflexionar sobre la igualdad de género, la soberanía emocional, y la diversidad cultural en las relaciones afectivas. A través de historias reales y análisis íntimos, el libro ofrece una puerta de entrada accesible y crítica al estudio de género, deseo y poder.

Objetivos de Aprendizaje

Al finalizar los módulos, se espera que los y las estudiantes sean capaces de:

- Analizar los roles de género y sus impactos en la vida afectiva.

- Identificar dinámicas de poder en las relaciones íntimas y en la sociedad.

- Comprender cómo el racismo, el machismo y la colonización afectan el amor y el deseo.

- Desarrollar pensamiento crítico y sensibilidad emocional a partir de relatos reales.

- Participar en conversaciones seguras e interseccionales sobre identidad, afecto y autonomía.

Módulos de Discusión

Cada módulo aborda un conjunto de temas, preguntas orientadoras y sugerencias para actividades reflexivas o colaborativas.

Módulo 1: El Cuerpo, el Terreno y la Primera Salida
(Basado en el Prólogo y el Capítulo 0)

Temas: Seguridad, Consentimiento, Memoria Femenina, Autonomía Corporal

Preguntas para dialogar:

- ¿Qué significa sentirse segura en una cita?

- ¿Por qué necesitamos hablar de "protocolos de seguridad" antes del amor?

- ¿Cómo las mujeres aprenden a sobrevivir en espacios de seducción?

- ¿Qué no ven (o no quieren ver) los hombres sobre el miedo que cargamos?

Actividad:

Escribe una carta a tu "yo adolescente" sobre lo que aprendiste sobre límites y cuidado personal.

Módulo 2: El Encanto como Máscara
(Capítulos como Stephan – El Galán Nigeriano o Savvas – La Trampa de la Sensibilidad Cultural)

Temas: Masculinidades Performativas, Manipulación Afectiva, Dulzura y Control

Preguntas para dialogar:

- ¿Cuándo el encanto se convierte en una estrategia de poder?

- ¿Qué tipo de "personaje" se espera que interpreten los hombres en la seducción?

- ¿Qué es el consentimiento emocional y cómo se rompe?

Actividad Creativa:

Representar una escena de coqueteo y analizar juntos/as los gestos, silencios y juegos de poder.

Módulo 3: Deseo, Cultura y la Trampa de la Exotización
(Capítulos como Ali – El Afgano-Alemán o Simone – La Francesa)

Temas: Raza y Deseo, Estereotipos Étnicos, Identidad Queer, Feminidad Libre

Preguntas para dialogar:

- ¿Te han deseado alguna vez por tu origen? ¿Cómo te hizo sentir?

- ¿Dónde está la línea entre admiración cultural y fetichismo?

- ¿Quién tiene derecho a ser deseado/a como persona completa?

Actividad Grupal:

Escoge una historia de amor de una serie, telenovela o reality show. Analiza las dinámicas de género, raza y poder que aparecen.

Módulo 4: Las Pruebas Invisibles – Masculinidades y Trabajo Emocional
(Capítulos como Ewan – El Escocés Enigmático o Phillip – El Sueño de Nieve)

Temas: Carga Mental, Silencios Masculinos, Cuidados Invisibles

Preguntas para dialogar:

• ¿Qué tareas emocionales se asignan (a menudo) a las mujeres sin que se note?

• ¿Qué significa poner "a prueba" a alguien en una relación? ¿Por qué lo hacemos?

• ¿Cómo puede cambiar la educación emocional de los hombres?

Ejercicio Reflexivo:

Describe un momento en que sentiste que diste más de lo que recibiste emocionalmente. ¿Cómo podrías haber actuado diferente?

Módulo 5: Libertad, Fe y lo Femenino como Fuerza
(Capítulos como Sri – El Uniforme de la Gracia o Simone – La Francesa)

Temas: Espiritualidad, Autonomía, Deseo Ético, Amor Elegido

Preguntas para dialogar:

• ¿Qué diferencia hay entre amar desde la libertad y desde la necesidad?

• ¿Es posible tener compromiso sin perder la individualidad?

• ¿Cómo influyen las creencias (religiosas, familiares o espirituales) en lo que entendemos por "amor verdadero"?

Actividad de Escritura:

Crea tu propio "contrato afectivo" con lo que tú necesitas, valoras y no estás dispuesta/o a negociar en una relación.

Sugerencias para Evaluación (flexible según edad)

• Diario personal: 5 entradas breves con reflexiones semanales.

• Ensayo argumentativo: Comparar una historia del libro con una película o canción que trate de amor y poder.

• Podcast escolar: Crear un episodio donde los/as estudiantes entrevisten personas reales sobre sus aprendizajes amorosos.

• Cartas colectivas: Redactar una carta a futuras generaciones sobre lo que significa amar con conciencia.

Lecturas Complementarias

• Todos deberíamos ser feministas – Chimamanda Ngozi Adichie

• El segundo sexo – Simone de Beauvoir

- La vida no es útil – Ailton Krenak

- Hombres explican cosas – Rebecca Solnit

- Mujeres, raza y clase – Angela Davis

Consejos para el/la Docente

- No se trata de confesión, sino de reflexión.

- Crear espacios seguros y sin juicio.

- Recordar que este libro no ofrece recetas, sino preguntas honestas.

- Adaptar el lenguaje si necesario, pero mantener la complejidad del tema.

"If you read all the way here,
maybe this book wasn't just about me.
Maybe it was about the part of you that still believes
love is worth learning — again, and again, and again."

Gratitude. Gratidão. Gratitud.

To bring this book into your classroom, workshop, or community:
niayara.com
IG: @theniayaraCopyright © 2025 Nia Yara

Published in English, Portuguese, and Spanish by Nia Yara.
Printed and distributed by Amazon KDP / IngramSpark
Website: www.niayara.com

First edition, 2025

For inquiries: emailniayara@gmail.com

If you enjoyed your purchase, please consider leaving a review on
amazon.com
Your opinion is important to us.

NIA YARA

www.ingramcontent.com/pod-product-compliance
Lightning Source LLC
Chambersburg PA
CBHW041819090426
42811CB00009B/1041